FREEDOMLAND

BY
AMY FREED

D1457455

★

★

DRAMATISTS
PLAY SERVICE
INC.

FREEDOMLAND
Copyright © 1999, Amy Freed

ALL RIGHTS RESERVED

SPECIAL NOTE

Playwrights Horizons, New York City, produced the World Premiere of
FREEDOMLAND off-Broadway in 1998-1999.
Tim Sanford, Artistic Director; Leslie Marcus, Managing Director.

Further developed and produced in 1998 at the Woolly Mammoth Theatre
Company, Washington D.C.
Howard Shalwitz, Artistic Director; Kevin Moore, Managing Director.

Commissioned and first produced by South Coast Repertory
David Emmes, Producing Artistic Director; Paula Tomei, Managing Director.

SPECIAL NOTE ON SONGS AND RECORDINGS

FREEDOMLAND was produced by Playwrights Horizons (Tim Sanford, Artistic Director; Leslie Marcus, Managing Director) in New York City, on October 17, 1998. It was directed by Howard Shalwitz; the set design was by Loy Arcenas; the costume design was by Candice Donnelly; the lighting design was by Christopher Akerlind; the original music and sound design were by Johnna Doty; and the production stage manager was Amanda W. Sloan. The cast was as follows:

SIG .... Veanne Cox
TITUS .... Jeff Whitty
POLLY .... Carrie Preston
NOAH .... Dakin Matthews
CLAUDE .... Robin Strasser
SETH .... Jeffrey Donovan
LORI .... Heather Goldenhersh

FREEDOMLAND was produced by South Coast Repertory (David Emmes, Producing Artistic Director; Martin Benson; Artistic Director; Paula Tomei, Managing Director) in Costa Mesa, California, on October 10, 1997. It was directed by David Emmes; the set design was by Michael C. Smith; the costume design was by Susan Denison Geller; the lighting design was by Peter Maradudin; the sound design was by B.C. Keller; the dramaturg was Jerry Patch; and the stage manager was Scott Harrison. The cast was as follows:

SIG .... Heather Ehlers
TITUS .... Maury Ginsberg
POLLY .... Annie LaRussa
NOAH .... Peter Michael Goetz
CLAUDE .... Karen Kondazian
SETH .... Simon Billig
LORI .... Erin J. O'Brien

3

CAST OF CHARACTERS

SIG — Thirty-seven years old. A successful painter of circus clowns. Rather glamorous. Acerbic. Her brittle exterior masks a passionate and vulnerable emotional core.

POLLY — Her sister, thirty-four. An unemployed Greek scholar. Dishevelled, honest and earnest.

SETH — Their brother, thirty-three. A survivalist. His hard life is starting to show. Physically rugged, threatening, but with an unexpected beauty or delicacy somewhere in him. Like his sisters, blazingly sincere.

NOAH — Their father, mid-sixties. A recently retired Professor of Comparative Religion. Brilliant, iconoclastic, lost. Hopeful but haunted. A stargazer.

CLAUDE — His wife, mid-fifties. A therapist. Seductive earth-mother. Self-obsessed, warm, scary.

TITUS — Writer for a visual-arts magazine. Late twenties. A shy, very smart egghead. Hip and geeky. Attractive, but doesn't know it.

LORI — Seth's girlfriend, twenty-five, six months pregnant. Could be quite pretty if she called attention to her looks in any way. Lori radiates simple goodness and knows more than she shows.

SETTING

The first scene takes place in an urban artist's loft. The remainder of the play takes place in an old house somewhere in New England. The time is contemporary. The play's actions take place over a single weekend.

FREEDOMLAND

ACT ONE

Scene 1

An eerie urban painting-studio. There are forms of clowns, heads, faces, dummies, circus fragments. Apparently, this is the painter's subject. Sig, in a paint-covered smock and old work-clothes, is showing her work to Titus, a magazine editor. He makes notes in a small reporter's notebook.

SIG. Number one-seventy-three. It's a very early painting but it's still one of my favorites. A little boy clown is in the rain under a dripping umbrella. All around him, the knees of the people rushing to work. He holds a crumpled handkerchief up to his little clown nose. His great big painted eyes are filled with wonder. He stands a little pigeon-toed as all of my children clowns do. One big shoe crosses the other, his little stockings are falling down — look, I get all teary just thinking about my clowns.
TITUS. Is — is — that one what I think it is?
SIG. It's Clowns Attending the Funeral of a Parakeet. With my work, you don't have to guess, Titus. You don't have to wonder if you're right, or wrong, are you getting it, are you too stupid. What is the "message" of the Clowns? I comfort. I care. *(They survey the painting.)*
TITUS. My sense — is that they KILLED that parakeet. As a kind of sacrifice.
SIG. Isn't that ridiculous.
TITUS. Well, look. Why is that one holding a pair of scissors?
SIG. Because they cut FLOWERS for the FUNERAL! For

God's Sake!

TITUS. The scissors are — bloody.

SIG. They are rusty! They are Hobos! What are they supposed to do! Go buy NEW scissors? They CAN'T! They live in BOXES! They have NOTHING!

TITUS. Very comforting.

SIG. Just what are you implying?

TITUS. Sentimentality as a form of Murderous Aggression! I have to tell you, I see a lot of new work but this is really twisted!

SIG. Twisted? Are you accusing my clown-babies of something dirty?

TITUS. Subversive! — unsettling! —

SIG. *(Over "unsettling.")* Look, Buddy. Why don't you just take your little notebook —

TITUS. *(Over "notebook.")* — overwhelmingly BRILLIANT!

SIG. — and have a look around? Make yourself at home. *(Pause.)*

TITUS. Can you tell me about your influences?

SIG. Oh, well. The great Walter Keene, the June Taylor Dancers, the Eisenhower years —

TITUS. What about your early life?

SIG. My memories are happy. Vague, but happy. I was a happy child. Something about a bunny.

TITUS. It seems there's a direct Rockwell reference —

SIG. Rockwell. What can one say. He's God.

TITUS. You meet him on his own level of expertise —

SIG. Yes, I've always tried —

TITUS. And then stand him on his head! — Post-narrative dislocation rises from these canvases like an airborne DISEASE! *(He makes a note.)*

SIG. Look Buster. I make a lot of MON-AY! I am NOT some misfit FREAK in TORMENT! America LOVES my clowns! The Japanese are buying them buy the hundreds! Senators! Tycoons! Dictators of Third-World COUNTRIES!

TITUS. Well. *(He notices a half-concealed painting.)*

SIG. No — that's not —

TITUS. Oh! It's still wet.

SIG. It's my own category, really. Something new. A Cautionary Portrait.

TITUS. *(Moved.)* That clown. There's something about her. She's really — beautiful.

SIG. *(Tightly.)* My sister Polly posed for it. A wistful little hobo-clown in baggy pants and a floppy hat stands on the train tracks. She clutches the remains of a cheese sandwich that she probably found in a garbage can near the station house — her ratty suitcase is bulging —

TITUS. With — what is that? Papers, it looks like?

SIG. Her Doctoral Dissertation.

TITUS. Her Doctoral Dissertation?

SIG. *(More controlled than fraught.)* Yes, she has left her studies and now stands on the train-tracks of life with a useless, unfinished Doctoral Dissertation. She is crying because she doesn't know which way to go — or if she should just lie down on the tracks. I take care of my sister. She lives here. Or did. She looked at her portrait for a long long time this morning and then she just took off.

TITUS. Where'd she go?

SIG. *(More fraught than controlled.)* Oh, probably back to Dad's. Yes, I believe that's where she's gone. HOME. Where you can eat whenever you like, if you can ever find any food. You can sleep late, all day if you want, and no one cares. Why, you can just sleep in a pile of rags in the attic like a PUPPY and no one bothers to get you up for school! HOME! Where you cried yourself sick for MOTHER but of course, she never came, having done the sensible thing and BOLTED years before —

TITUS. She —

SIG. *(Continuous — In Full Cry.)* — Home! — where you dressed yourself and your brother and sister the best you could — and you trundled off to school looking like the GISH sisters with your hair on end, and no one noticed, no one combed you, no one washed your neck!

TITUS. You —

SIG. *(Continuous.)* I was the strong one! But Polly is hapless. Polly needs tough love. And I promised Mother that I'd always look after her. Come on, Titus. We're going to Dad's.

TITUS. OK.

Scene 2

Noah's house. The "great room" of a colonial dwelling. It's been added to over time — vintage post-and-beam construction is somewhere visible, and a large fireplace of more recent date. The space continues into a large kitchen, part of which may be visible. Transoms or multipaned window banks have been added. In a recent addition, Noah has added a hinged trapdoor to the roof. There's a ladder that leads up to it. Part of the sky is always visible. The feeling of the interior is both messy and attractive. There are places to nest, read, sleep, or sprawl. There's also a big rectory table that gets pressed into service for company. Artifacts, many of them religious, from around the world, nest in alcoves or in the numerous bookshelves. The rough dignity of a primitive crucifix, or the unexpected energy of a painted mask help to organize the room. There are family artifacts, dating back to the house's origins. There are hundreds of books. Late-afternoon light fills the room. Polly stands downstage, sets down her suitcase. She hugs her baggy sweater for comfort. Noah joins her at window.

NOAH. *(Gazing at the sky.)* On an afternoon like this, at the age of forty-seven, Great-Grand-Uncle Sirius Underfinger had a vision of Paradise. It came to him in a spent corn-field outside of Allentown. He saw the clouds roll back. Elijah — descending down a ramp of sunlight like a Las Vegas Showgirl. Great-Grand Uncle was shown the City made of Diamonds, where the streets were paved with precious gemstones. Imagine. The incredible vulgarity of a Heaven made of Jewels. They couldn't have imagined Beverly Hills, in those days. Or the opulent glister of Park Avenue. But here I am — at the end of a long line of reformers and celestial gazers and where is it I gaze? Into the windows of the new Starbuck's erected on the Old Post Road and I imagine Heaven as simply —

a spent corn-field.

POLLY. Dad, I've — had a little situation.

NOAH. *(Distracted.)* They ALL saw it that way, you know. The reformers, and their City Made of Gold — *(Crosses to book-laden desk.)* — where is my *Pilgrim's Progress,* it was lying open here —

POLLY. *(Following.)* — do you still mind when I call you "Dad" ... or would you prefer "artist formerly known as Dad" ... or should we go with — "Dad" — kind of in quotes?

NOAH. *(Peers at her.)* I would prefer Noah, but do what you need to do. "Dad" in quotes would be ok. As long as we both understand — the — the *implication* of the quotes.

POLLY. All right.

NOAH. *(Finding book.)* HERE it is. Maybe it was only money they were dreaming of after all. Bunyan and his brethren. "Prophets" of "profit."

POLLY. *(Brightly.)* Speaking of "money" —

NOAH. *(Crossing to window.)* — where the HELL is it all COMING from? Look at that next door. A million dollar tear-down. And he can't be more than thirty! Well. He's got a tear-down, I've got a fall-down! What's the damn difference. *(Crosses to ladder.)* Oh — look. I've cut a hole in the ceiling and fitted it with a trap door. How's that! You can see the stars at night.

POLLY. *(Desperate.)* — THINGS AREN'T GOING SO WELL — "DAD." *(Pause.)*

NOAH. Ah — after all, what is "well," "Polly?"

POLLY. No. You don't have to put quotes around "Polly." Because I really AM "Polly."

NOAH. That's what you think. You should come up on the rooftop with me, Daughter, and listen to the voices in the wind. Shall we have a real drink?

POLLY. I — have something to tell you. I've joined AA.

NOAH. *(Devastated.)* Oh, God! What did I do to turn you into a drunk! No, don't TELL me — I can't recall a thing. *(Heading for the door.)*

POLLY. Wait, Noah, I —

NOAH. *(Returning.)* — my peace is shaky, Polly, but I was almost there! You destroy my almost complete detachment — eight years of Sufi circle dancing down the damn drain! — Why did you come back here! —

POLLY. I'M NOT A DRUNK, "DAD!" I don't even like the taste! I just like going to AA is all. *(Pause.)*

NOAH. Oh.

POLLY. *(Painfully enthused, not quite daring to look at him.)* The meetings have really been HELPING me. And — to be able to CALL someone at two in the morning, if you need to — and they'll pick up the phone and TALK to you. Really TALK! *(Noah is becoming oddly distracted.)* I say, look, Susan — Susan, that's my sponsor — I'm sorry to call you so late. She says — that's OK. What's going on. Well, I say, I went to this party and there was ALCOHOL there — she says, did you DRINK — and I say NO, which is totally TRUE — and she says, GOOD FOR YOU! GOOD JOB! *(An outburst.)* And I feel BETTER about myself!! In a way, that's what I've always NEEDED!! Someone who was willing to really pay —

NOAH. *(Jumps. Loudly.)* Ow! DAMN it!

POLLY. *(Scared.)* What's the matter?

NOAH. *(Very alarmed.)* Something just bit me in the ass! I don't know what it was, though. It's been happening. I can almost SEE it — a shape, a looming, an INTELLIGENCE and then WHAP! There it goes! *(He eyes the air, apprehensive.)*

POLLY. *(Shaky.)* Well ... retirement is hard ... "Dad."

NOAH. Retirement is easy! It's what's NEXT is hard. Let me tell you. The Last Judgment makes a tax-audit look like your sixth birthday party. *(Pause.)*

POLLY. I lost my job at Animal-Land.

NOAH. — DOWNsized by the relentless spread of Globalization.

POLLY. I bounced from one lousy temp-job to another.

NOAH. — Screw the worker who MADE them! Oh, that makes me angry!

POLLY. I couldn't pay my rent, I had to stay with Sig. She made me stretch her canvases, and run her shows —

NOAH. I don't really GET your sister. Now what is she all about?

POLLY. — so can I stay here for a while? I just need a quiet place where I can THINK and get my — *(She stops.)*

NOAH. Wonderful! What a good idea!

POLLY. All right. I'll leave.

10

NOAH. It's not that I don't want you. It's just that THINGS are going on.

POLLY. What kind of things?

NOAH. Comparative Religion Professor — who did I think I was, Comparing when I should have been Professing! I might as well have spent my life as a professor of SWIMMING! Because there is nothing for it but to IMMERSE. And now I can. Because there is nothing to harass me any more.

POLLY. That's wonderful!

NOAH. No, it's not, it's terrible. You know, your whole life, the world torments you. Plucking at your time, your resources, your sanity. Then suddenly, like wolves around the campfire, it falls back. The phone doesn't ring. You don't need voice-mail. You're granted peace. A respite. You taste metal in your mouth and you realize that you're afraid. They finally give you time because your time is almost out.

POLLY. That's terrible —

NOAH. Well, it was, but something has started to happen. Oh, Polly, you've got here in the nick of time itself.

POLLY. What do you mean?

NOAH. After years of studying God, as if the MASTER were a subject for Mastery — SOMETHING — has suddenly started to study ME.

POLLY. — what?

NOAH. An attention — as powerful as a blanket. Can't you feel it?

POLLY. No —

NOAH. The air is almost speaking. Shh. Listen — *(They listen.)* Did you hear? Could you hear? Unstructured sound. The place where language stops is the place where language begins. And who, or what, begins it. Who sets the music — who. who. who. who. who? *(His attention rolling inward —)*

POLLY. *(Frightened.)* Stop! Please — ! I can't do those LISTENING things, "Dad" —

NOAH. Anyway, of course you'll stay. As long as you like. It's all settled.

POLLY. *(Crossing up to the daybed with her suitcase.)* It would give me a chance to finish my dissertation —

NOAH. From Disserare — to examine. *What* will you examine?

POLLY. — the secret lives of the Women of *The Iliad.*

NOAH. You know, I can't seem to recall too many —

POLLY. Well, that's the point. Oh, it's so EASY to get sidetracked by the MALE side of the epic, you know, all those warriors and their bloody feats of courage —

NOAH. *(Very interested.)* — all done, you know, without any hope of immortal life, or heaven.

POLLY. *(Not quite hearing him.)* — oiling their golden bodies, at night — in the flare and flicker of the campfires —

NOAH. *(More to himself.)* I mean, because what WAS Hades —

POLLY. *(Becoming aroused.)* — binding their massive thighs with thongs of leather —

NOAH. *(To himself.)* — nothing to DIE for certainly —

POLLY. *(To herself.)* — massaging the rippling shoulders of their comrades —

NOAH. *(In awe.)* No "Salvation," just a promise of honor …

POLLY. *(In heat.)* — striding naked into the field, their rippling buttocks lifting and flexing like the snorting stallions of the Gods — GOD! where are all the MEN these days! Where are all the MEN!!

NOAH. Polly?

POLLY. *(Embarrassed.)* Well. See, I've just made my own point. It's so easy to overlook the WOMEN! They are UNSUNG!

NOAH. What were all the gals up to?

POLLY.   Exactly! What was THEIR epic! And when I find THEIRS, I will find Ours. Mine. Towards a Female Heroics.

NOAH. What a good idea. And what have you got so far.

POLLY. Well, it's GESTATING, right now. I just need to crawl into a corner somewhere and give BIRTH to it.

NOAH. Wonderful. Do you know what, I was just reading, in the Sunday *Book Review* — where is it, now. *(Finding it.)* The Ancient Sumerians have — seventy different words for — "Unemployable." God. Isn't that fascinating. Look here, Polly — they've just found a scroll. *(Reading it.)* An instruction to overseers. Gahash. Cannot follow instruction. Ga-HA-hash. Rises at noon. Oh, this one is good. Hagamash. Never comes back from lunch.

POLLY. *(Taking it.)* HANTA-mash. "Not having even a pot to boil barley in." *(Whimpering.)* I AM in a state of TOTAL Hanta-mash.

NOAH. The Slough of Despond. Don't I know it. Oh, what fun

to have you back. *(Noah's wife, Claude, enters. Early fifties. She's a therapist.)*

CLAUDE. Polly! It's Polly! Welcome!

POLLY. Hi, Claude.

CLAUDE. Oh, Baby. You're welcome to call me Mom.

POLLY. But you're not my Mom, Claude.

CLAUDE. You really hurt me when you say that.

POLLY. Our real Mom made us call her Jane.

NOAH. Why did she do that? It wasn't her name, was it?

CLAUDE. *(Helpful.)* You can call me "Jane" if it helps you heal your mother-wound.

NOAH. Where were you, Honey?

CLAUDE. *(Serene.)* Group! I had Group.

NOAH. Wow. It was group night again. Time — flies. "Time." "flies." *(They consider this.)* Wow.

CLAUDE. Wow.

NOAH. How was it?

CLAUDE. *(Smiles at him.)* Fantastic. The sex was fantastic.

NOAH. *(Smiles at her.)* Good. Good.

CLAUDE. *(Smiles at Polly.)* Polly, I go to this incredible group. We're all therapists. Well, last week we all got naked together and sat in this hot tub — You know, I thought I was through my barriers, but I'm not young and to sit with these strangers, with this old body just hanging out there — I'm not from California, you know, and I felt so accepted! and they held me and I cried, and I had a realization. *(She closes her eyes and centers herself.)* That I feel utterly alone unless I've shared orgasm with another human being. *(She smiles at Noah. He smiles back. A moment. Polly is frozen, but fascinated.)*

NOAH. The Divine Conversation.

CLAUDE. It's transforming my work with my patients. Hey, I interrupted you two. *(Focuses intently on Polly, draws her over to the couch.)* Polly — where are you in your process?

NOAH. *(To himself.)* — Incredible. Why criminalize … Love.

POLLY. *(Giving way.)* My whole life is just going to Hell!

NOAH. *(To himself.)* Our whole civilization built on Guilt and Damnation!

POLLY. I feel like I can't really —

13

CLAUDE. *(Overlapping, helpful, to Polly.)* Function?

POLLY. *(Feeling worse.)* — or get my dissertation off the ground because I'm in such doubt about my —

CLAUDE. *(Quickly and gently.)* Intelligence —

POLLY. *(Feeling worse.)* — and all that I really want to do is prove to myself that I can be —

CLAUDE. — taken seriously! Not seen as a ... half-baked ... sort of person?

POLLY. *(Feeling worse.)* And I have no self-worth at all because —

CLAUDE. *(Helpfully.)* — your real mother left you — !

POLLY. *(Struggling for breath.)* And I don't have any —

CLAUDE. Money!! Well, I know. Yes. These are real feelings. *(Polly is hyperventilating and waving her arms.)* Yes, that's right. Breathe. Breathe.

POLLY. I'm BAD! I'm BAD!

CLAUDE. Whose voice is that. Saying —

NOAH. *(To himself. A meditation.)* The sense — of "Original Sin!"

CLAUDE. *(To Polly.)* — "Bad!"

POLLY. I don't KNOW!!

NOAH. *(To himself.)* Why "Seven?" Why "Deadly?" What ARE they, anyway? Sloth —

POLLY. *(Collapsing — to Claude.)* Well, I haven't had much get up and go —

CLAUDE. *(To Polly.)* Tell me.

NOAH. *(To himself.)* Gluttony —

POLLY. *(Ravenous — to Claude.)* And I feel like all I want to do is EAT —

CLAUDE. *(To Polly.)* Are you having sex?

NOAH. *(To himself.)* Lust —

POLLY. *(Writhing — to Claude.)* I haven't had a date in three years!

NOAH. *(To himself.)* Wrath — the germ of Murder!

POLLY. *(Furious — to Claude.)* I could kill my sister. Its HER fault.

NOAH. *(To himself.)* Pride —

POLLY. *(Swaggering — to Claude.)* — of course she's a pompous idiot who thinks she better than me — ME — ME!!

NOAH. *(Noticing something.)* Don't you notice something?

POLLY. What?

NOAH. — Something? Something funny? — *(Pause. He's sud-*

denly bitten by something huge and invisible.) OW!!!

POLLY. "Dad!" What's wrong!

NOAH. *(Grabbing himself in the ass.)* Damn it! What IS that! *(A peal of thunder.)*

CLAUDE. *(Serene.)* It's going to rain again. Shut the trapdoor, Noah.

POLLY. *(In disarray.)* I'm — I'm not feeling very well. Do you think, would you mind if I went and took a bath? I think I need a long hot bath.

CLAUDE. Want me to take a bath with you and we can really talk?

POLLY. NO!

CLAUDE. That's totally cool. I love our big bathtub. I love to float in it for hours. Like a fetus.

POLLY. I just thought a bath would be nice —

CLAUDE. Yes.

POLLY. Is there a phone?

CLAUDE. Use the phone in my bedroom if you want a private conversation. There's a phone in the bathroom but we took the doors off the bathroom.

POLLY. *(Panicked.)* Why? Why did you do that?

CLAUDE. *(Serene.)* To release shame. But if you aren't ready for it, use the toilet in the Winnebago. Everything in its time. Late Harvest, Great Harvest. *(Rain begins and more low thunder.)* Listen.

POLLY. Once upon a time I had hoped to harvest more than the ability to shit in public! But maybe its right. Maybe that's me. Maybe that's the best one could expect of me. Oh, God! Good night "Dad," good night "Claude" it's very nice — to be home. *(She exits, weeping.)*

NOAH. *(Sits, reflectively.)* What it is to be ... Waste. To BE waste matter. What is that. Well, it's — it's — to compost oneself, isn't it. To understand that to fall apart as "Shit" is to be reborn as "Roses."

CLAUDE. *(Settling in for the evening.)* She's doing very well. I love to see your children.

NOAH. I've had the strangest dreams — like dead fingers pulling at my hair all night — I wake up and its knotted like string. It feels like something may happen.

15

Scene 3

Next morning. The daybed in the living room. Polly is in a sleeping bag.

POLLY. *(Yawning.)* Rosy-fingered Dawn touches the eyes of the slumbering Acheans. They arise from their smoldering campfires. *(Thoughtful.)* In preparation for their ritual baths — they are ... Naked. *(Pause.)* The smoky air fills with the sound of coarse jokes and the snapping of many towels. Laughter rises like the barking of — young — lions. Meanwhile, back in the female quarters — the early-rising and industrious women are ... cranking up their looms. Cranking up their LOOMS! God. Images. Images. Where are our images of Female Power! *(Claude enters in a nightgown and a black bondage mask.)*
CLAUDE. Do you want breakfast?
POLLY. Oh God!
CLAUDE. *(Realizing.)* Oh. One of my patients gave it to me. I tell you what, I like the way it feels. Everything all tight, firm, tucked away. My head like a little darning-egg. And so private! You can't tell what I'm thinking back here. I could be anyone.
POLLY. You're scaring me!
CLAUDE. *(Pleased.)* Am I? Am I really? *(Taking it off.)* Your brother's downstairs.
POLLY. Seth? What's he doing here.
CLAUDE. I don't know, but he and your father are doing a purge-the-past-process-thing already.
POLLY. Why don't you just call it purgatory. That's what it is, purgatory.
CLAUDE. Seth has a girl with him. She's pregnant. *(Noah and Seth, enter, shadowboxing. A timid backwoods-woman, Lori, following.)*
SETH. I'M YOUNGER AND STRONGER THAN YOU ARE NOAH — I COULD TEAR YOUR FUCKING HEAD OFF!!
SETH and NOAH. HAHAHAHAHA

16

SETH. I CAME ALL THE WAY DOWN HERE JUST TO STRAIGHTEN YOU THE FUCK OUT, YOU ADDLE-BRAIN OLD SMACK-HEAD!

SETH and NOAH. HOHOHOHOHO

SETH. YOU DON'T SCARE ME — I'M NOT PUTTING UP WITH YOUR INTELLECTUAL BULLSHIT! ACT! ANY MORE.

SETH and NOAH. HAHAHAHA

NOAH. Wow. I'm really winded.

SETH. Had you going, "Dad" —

NOAH. I knew you were fooling —

SETH. No, you didn't, I saw the fear in your eyes, you old FUCK —

NOAH. Oh, I don't think so —

SETH. Oh, I think so — "DAD!"

NOAH. "SON!"

SETH and NOAH. HAHAHAHAH! *(They beat each other on the backs in hostile embrace. Seth breaks away.)*

SETH. Hello, Polly. What are you doing here?

POLLY. Well, I've decided to rediscover my roots as a scholar, and —

SETH. Out of work, huh. I wouldn't have showed up if I thought Polly was going to be here! *(Punching her painfully on the arm.)* I mean who wants to listen to a lot of BULLSHIT about the BRONZE AGE — !

SETH and NOAH. HAHAHAHAHAH!

POLLY. *(Scandalized.)* "Dad!" Oh, why do I even bother! Why don't I just — (kill myself —)

SETH. *(Overlap.)* Hey Noah — guess what. I'm really getting into smelting!

NOAH. SMELTING! Neat!

SETH. *(Going to Lori.)* This is Lori, my partner.

CLAUDE. Well, HELLO there! I see congratulations are in order.

LORI. Well, not yet, but soon!

CLAUDE. Welcome, Seth. *(Starts towards him.)*

SETH. *(Friendly.)* Keep your fucking distance.

CLAUDE. Cool!

SETH. Well, Lori. This place was built by my great-great-grandfather. Built it with his bare hands.

LORI. Wow.

SETH. Look at these planks. Twelve-inch heart-cut old pine planks.

NOAH. That's right, Son. You'd never see this today —

SETH. Handhewn eight by eight support posts —

NOAH. Not anymore.

POLLY. Really? You wouldn't see a —

CLAUDE. Oh, no. You know they wanted to do a piece for American Home but —

LORI. This is so nice!

SETH. Lori, these old walls still got chinks to allow a musket through. Jesus CHRIST! Where are the CHINKS, DAD! you didn't plaster em over, did you?

CLAUDE. Oh, no, Seth —

NOAH. No, no. Hell, no. Right over there, Seth. Behind the picture of Whozis.

SETH. *(Crossing to wall.)* See, Lori?

LORI. Wow —

NOAH. Just two rooms, once upon a time — one to live in — and one to be laid out in.

SETH. *(Joining him.)* Let you just die at home back then.

NOAH. When Great-Great-Grandfather Obadiah died, the whole house shook with his struggles —

SETH. *(Slapping Noah on the back.)* Right before the end he sat bolt upright and he said Lord!

SETH and NOAH. I'm coming through — I'm coming through!

NOAH. *(Slapping Seth on the back.)* Now they take you to a funeral parlor and paint you up like something out of a Barcelona Brothel —

SETH. Fuck the fucking funeral industry —

NOAH. That's right.

SETH. *(Overlap.)* A plain plank box in a fucking hole in the fucking garden.

NOAH. What the hell else does a man need?

SETH. Not a damn thing.

NOAH. Not a damn thing. *(Pause.)*

POLLY. Well, Lori, what did you do in your past life to end up

18

with my brother?

SETH. *(To Polly.)* Shut up.

LORI. Actually, Seth rescued me from my past life. My past life being my situation only seven months ago. You see I was married to a very abusive man.

CLAUDE and POLLY and NOAH. *(In order.)* Oh? Really? Wow.

LORI. It was awful! I had terrible low self-esteem. And to escape my home life I married Atlas.

NOAH and CLAUDE and POLLY. *(In order.)* Really? Ahh. Wow.

LORI. *(With mounting enthusiasm.)* Well, talk about out of the frying pan into the fire! You see, Atlas worked on the boats, and because of that life style as well as his country of origin where it was considered perfectly OK to beat your wives and girlfriends, oh, I had a terrible time.

POLLY and CLAUDE and NOAH. *(In order.)* Yikes! Whew! Wow!

LORI. Working as a barmaid when I could stay off the dope —

CLAUDE. *(Quickly and quietly.)* Noah, are we ordering in tonight?

SETH. What the FUCK is wrong with her?

CLAUDE. Oh … I'm sorry, Lori —

LORI. Oh, that's all right. I'm that way myself sometimes. Anyway, Seth says he doesn't care whose baby it is and all that matters is that we're family. *(Pause.)*

NOAH. *(Jovial with dread.)* Good! Well isn't this fantastic. My "off"-"spring" — springing back at me like the jaws of a loaded wolf-trap — All of my salmon — coming for me — leaping back down the stream at me, nipping at my jugular —

POLLY. Well, except that wild horses couldn't drag Sig up here. That's one reason that I'm up here.

CLAUDE. *(To Lori.)* I never get to see Seth anymore! What fun!

LORI. Oh, I've been dying to meet Seth's family —

NOAH. *(Enthusiastically, trying to make his escape.)* Well. I 've got to get back up to the roof. Liberty Hall everyone! Amuse yourselves — and I'm sure we'll all bump into each other over the weekend.

SETH. I'm going to Poughkeepsie to take care of some business. I thought I'd leave Lori here for a while.

CLAUDE. We could sit in the tub and do facials.

LORI. That would be wonderful! Do you have hot water?

19

CLAUDE. You just come with me. *(Claude and Lori exit. Seth blocks Noah's escape to the roof-ladder.)*

SETH. *(Provocative.)* Hey, Noah. New Tools.

NOAH. Me too.

SETH. Tractor. This spring.

NOAH. *(Hackles rising.)* How many cylinders.

SETH. Twelve!! Spirit-Drive! Rigged up a snowplow attachment.

NOAH. Good. Good. Jigsaw. Since you last.

SETH. Table saw. Wood drill —

NOAH. — really! Terrific. Plack-Master —

SETH. — Skill-Drill, Black and Decker. Five-point, diamond-tooled! Heavy-gauge drill press!

NOAH. Trash-compactor — !!

SETH. Old hand-grinder-joist-turner —

NOAH. Corrugated punch metal press — junkyard resurrection — works like a fucking dream!!

SETH. Great. Check it out later. Got to see a man about two bucks worth of ordinary garden supply substance could blow your fucking flower beds to Mars!!

SETH and NOAH. HAHAHAHAHAHA! *(They pound each other on the back.)*

NOAH. Fantastic!

SETH. Great. So long. *(Exits.)*

NOAH. Well. Good. Good GOOD good good.

POLLY. *(Very excited.)* What was that?

NOAH. It was the theatre of MEN. We communicated that we were willing to role up our sleeves and tackle. Machinery. God. The mechanism of the universe. Uh oh. Here it comes. *(Grabs his ass.)* Man! That HURT! Well. I'm off to fix something. To tinker. Putter. Meditate on man's role in the cosmic turning of the wheels. Maybe take a look at that damn vacuum cleaner. *(Exits.)*

POLLY. *(Seizing a pancake turner.)* Andromache wishes it could be HER out there wielding the two-sided battle ax — wearing the terrible bright war-helmet with the nodding plumes. Testing herself in the cauldron of the Gods! *(Pause.)* But she'll never go. Never never never! Because she doesn't have any BALLS! No BALLS AT ALL!!! *(She runs off.)*

Scene 4

Sig enters the kitchen area, Titus in tow.

SIG. Well, this is it, Titus, the old homestead. Nothing's changed. My God. How strange. I can still almost smell that after-school smell, hot from the oven —
TITUS. Your mother making cookies — ?
SIG. Mother burning family records. Rocking and weeping as she fed the flames, smoke billowing out of the broiler. Birth certificates, Seth's science report.
TITUS. Why? Why did she burn them?
SIG. She had a sort of predilection for anguish. It was her gift. Mother didn't know if the glass was half empty or half full. But she DID know that the glass itself was some kind of a demonic illusion — at least that was how she always explained it to us when we were small. *(Pause.)* My God, I think that sandwich was rotting on the hearth the last time I was here.
TITUS. All these books — there must be thousands of books!
SIG. My father the professor.
TITUS. What's all this?
SIG. Aryuvedic medicine. For balancing Prana.
TITUS. And this?
SIG. Homeopathic remedies — for restoring the natural harmonies of the body.
TITUS. And these?
SIG. Percodan, Valium, and Xanax. Polly! *(Claude and Lori are heard offstage.)*
CLAUDE. *(Offstage.)* I was a practicing Sufi then, had been ever since Bennington — and then I — *(They enter. Lori looks dazed. They are wearing towels.)* Sigrid, well, Hi! Hello, Welcome — ! *(She extends her hand, her towel slips, somewhat.)* Oops, excuse me. I have my period and I'm so spacey — I'm FIFTY you'd think it would STOP already — but no — everything's achy, my breasts

21

are so swollen. Lori and I are hungry — we thought we'd rustle up some lunch. It's so HOT! I've simply got to get out of this towel. *(She flaps her towel open and shut. Goes up to refrigerator, opens the door and continues to flap.)*

SIG. Well, Titus, welcome to the bosoms of the family.

TITUS. Yes. Fine. Whatever.

SIG. That's my dad's wife, Claude.

LORI. I'm Lori. I'm Seth's partner.

SIG. You must be new.

LORI. Oh, just a few months, but it sure feels like longer!

CLAUDE. *(Finding chips.)* Anyone want chocolate chips?

SIG. No chips, no thank you, Claude. I'm making a pot of coffee, now. Just a pot of coffee.

CLAUDE. *(Excited.)* What fun! We'll have chocolate chips and coffee! Titus, where are you from? Is this your first visit to Cobb's Landing?

TITUS. Yes, Ma'am.

LORI. I'm going to get dressed, excuse me.

SIG. *(Agitated.)* Will someone explain the attraction of all that armpit hair to me?

CLAUDE. Oh, Sigrid. That is a lovely girl. She's lovely.

SIG. *(More agitated.)* That kind of thing, it's like a YETI or a YAK or something. Why do people DO that?

CLAUDE. Do you think she's lovely, Titus?

TITUS. I'm sure, Ma'am.

CLAUDE. Go to her. Follow her. Act. It's OK to act.

SIG. For Christ's sake CLAUDE!!

CLAUDE. Anyway, you don't care, do you? Sigrid. Are you in love with him?

SIG. All right.

CLAUDE. Did I say something?

TITUS. This is a nice house you have here.

SIG. Great. Great, Claude. Just say anything. ANYTHING!

CLAUDE. *(Apologetic.)* You know, I did this to her the last time she was here, she was struggling with her bulimia —

SIG. What the hell is the matter with you!!

CLAUDE. *(Quietly.)* I'm sorry, Sigrid, but Noah and I totally disclose. We are into Truth here. *(Pause.)*

SIG. They're "into" Truth. They're INTO TRUTH! Well, Why don't you go put your CLOTHES on because your BODY is SCARING the GUESTS!

CLAUDE. *(With dignity.)* Thank you for trusting me with your pain. I'm going to give you some private space now. *(She withdraws.)*

SIG. I'm sorry Titus. I believe I forgot myself.

TITUS. No, no — *(Polly enters, in pyjamas, eating something.)*

POLLY. Oh no.

SIG. Get your suitcase.

POLLY. You think I'm going back with you, you're crazy.

SIG. Yes yes yes.

POLLY. No, I really mean it — find yourself another lab assistant, Dr. Clownenstein. Go get yourself another hunchback. I'm through.

SIG. Get your stuff. We'll talk in the car. C'mon, Hon.

POLLY. Why are you calling me Hon. You never called me Hon in your life. Your place is weird. You're weird. Your paintings give me nightmares. Red noses, whiteface — all of them doing things to each other with GLOVES on so they won't leave PRINTS —

TITUS. Oh, Man. That's really incredible! The metaphoric resonance of the gloves. It's so you won't be incriminated by PRINTS! That's good!

POLLY. Who is this guy?

SIG. This is Titus. I've got some very good news. Titus is doing a story on me for the *New Arts Journal.* A cover story.

POLLY. Oh. God. Really?

SIG. Yes. I'm going to be VERY well known. What was that funny word you used, Titus?

TITUS. Famous?

SIG. That's the one! *(Singing.)* I'm going to be famous, rich and famous rich and famous, I'm going to be famous — Isn't that great, Hon? Isn't that a fun suprise?

POLLY. *(Hyperventilating.)* Hee Hee Hee!

TITUS. Does Polly have asthma?

SIG. No, no, no. It's just LIFE — Polly has trouble accepting life —

POLLY. HEEE! — not — HEE! TRUE!

SIG. So she makes herself turn BLUE in the FACE! Here, Honey, let me help.

POLLY. *(Stops gasping. Bitterly —)* Don't you TOUCH me — !

After I served as your GO-fer, your unpaid SLAVE!

SIG. What!?

POLLY. — to find myself pilloried and mocked in that grotesque DEPICTION of me!

SIG. Not grotesque! CONCERNED! A CONCERNED depiction of you!

POLLY. How dare you portray me as some pathetic little ragged Weirdo with no LIFE!

SIG. LOOK at yourself!

POLLY. What?

SIG. It's two o'clock in the afternoon.

POLLY. So?

SIG. You're still in your pajamas. And What Do We Say To Ourselves When That Happens?

POLLY. I don't know — I —

SIG. Oh, I think you DO know. Because we PRACTICED. We say, am I sick?

POLLY. This is —

SIG. AM I SICK!?

POLLY. No — !!?

SIG. Am I — THREE?

POLLY. No — !!?

SIG. Am I in an INSTITUTION of some sort?

SIG. Not YET — !   POLLY. No!

SIG. Then get dressed!

POLLY. You're so MEAN to me!

SIG. MEAN! For taking you into my life, when you were out of work and out of money!

POLLY. I answered your mail! Did your laundry! Took out your garbage! —

SIG. We had a wonderful time together, Titus — we watched movies, we baked cookies, I introduced Polly to all of my friends! We had such fun —

POLLY. She only has one friend, Titus, if you could call her DOG-walker a —

SIG. — how Polly would regale us all with her "studies" — of, what is it THIS week, Honey, household tips of Old Troy?

POLLY. What a laughable misrepresentation. Ha ha ha. *(Crossing*

24

to Titus.) My thesis — is about the nature of the warrior motif.

SIG. Polly likes pro-wrestling.

POLLY. *(To Titus.)* It's about the cult of the body as a pointer towards transcendence.

SIG. Polly likes the BIG boys.

TITUS. *(Fumbling.)* Um, do you have a title?

POLLY. "Simile as Metaphor." I'm appropriating the phallocentric projection of the vagina as the wound. All veiled warrior-speak — like, "I'm going to tear you a new asshole," for example, reflects the male longing to become female. *(She beams at him.)*

TITUS. Wow. I — I — never thought of that.

POLLY. All the way back in the Bronze Age. All through the *Iliad* you can feel the longing of the men to become women.

SIG. At the same time that Polly DREAMS of finding her very own Agamemnon, she is jealous of his POWER and longs to put him in a DRESS.

POLLY. *(Turning on her.)* My SISTER'S work, on the other hand, reflects the narcissistic loneliness of the ax-murderer —

SIG. How funny. Shut up.

POLLY. Yes, Titus, have you ever seen Sig's Pre-Clown work?

TITUS. No!

SIG. — art-school scribblings —

POLLY. — a big Pre-Clown period. Oh yes.

TITUS. Can I see —

SIG. I burned them all. They are destroyed.

POLLY. Portraits. Monumental, idealized portraits.

SIG. I was very young. I —

POLLY. *(Overlap with "very young.")* Adolf Hitler!

SIG. NO! *(Sig starts for Polly. Polly evades her, and drops to the floor to demonstrate —)*

POLLY. — sits shyly in a field and gazes into the distance in a virtuoso and PSYCHOTIC tribute to Andrew Wyeth! She called it *Christina Dreams of Taking Over the World!* *(She flashes a Nazi salute.)*

TITUS. Oh, Man!

SIG. Polly. If you do not stop I will stop you.

POLLY. *(Evades her.)* Ghengis Khan! Lizzie Borden — VERY bloody and ascending to heaven! They were powerful, unsettling, and terribly unpopular. Which was why she sold out, abandoned her original and unsavory depths, paddled for the shallows, and started to paint CLOWNS!

SIG. Yes. Sigrid is a SHALLOW SELLOUT, her income is in SIX figures. Polly is DEEP and full of INTEGRITY. Her income is in NO figures. *(Polly begins to claw the air.)* The question is - if the world rewards those who give it what it NEEDS — WHO NEEDS POLLY!

POLLY. Stop — stop — I'm having spatial disorientation —

TITUS. Here. Sit down — put your head down — *(He helps her to the footstool.)*

POLLY. Oh, thank you. What's your name, again?

TITUS. Titus.

POLLY. Hi.

TITUS. I think what you said about the *Iliad* is really intriguing. Of course! Helen of Troy!! SHE was a woman.

POLLY. Well, exactly!

TITUS. And Athena! Wisdom and War —

POLLY. And Achilles' mother — Thetis —

TITUS. That would be interesting, a thesis on Thetis —

POLLY. HAHAHAHA

TITUS. HAHAHAHA

SIG. What is this — the dating game? Polly, I care about you. That's why we're here. That's why we're having this little talk. I'm tired of you feeling like shit.

POLLY. That's not why we're having this talk. *You* feel like shit.

SIG. No, *you* feel like shit.

POLLY. You know what? You have no idea what other people feel like. Because you're —

SIG. DON'T you call me —

POLLY. Insane.

SIG. — DAMN it. I am not insane!

POLLY. Deep down inside Sig isn't really sure if other people exist or if she dreamed them all UP!

SIG. I — COMMAND you to stop talking.

POLLY. She thinks she made the whole WORLD up inside her head! — she's completely self-obsessed!

SIG. You little failure. You hateful little person.

26

POLLY. At heart, she's suicidal, Titus!

SIG. Bullshit!

POLLY. Every time she comes home she tries to jump off the roof!

SIG. What ridiculous LIES!

POLLY. And then she doesn't remember anything.

SIG. Absurd idiotic childish DRIVEL!! Little FREAK!

POLLY. Freak? Freak? Well, well, well. If we're going to invoke the BIG-top, let's talk about your CLOWNS!

SIG. Don't you DARE talk to me about my clowns!!

TITUS. Talk about the clowns!

SIG. You don't understand me. You're too SICK to understand me.

POLLY. *(Softly.)* The clowns are starting to TURN on you, Sig. Aren't they.

SIG. Oh, how —

POLLY. They come for you at night, don't they.

SIG. That is so —

POLLY. *(Gently.)* Do you hear MUSIC, Sig? *(Sig freezes.)* OOM pah pah, OOM pah pah! Secret music inside your head? You don't have to tell me, I know. OOM pah pah OOM pah pah! You think I don't notice you, swaying in time, when you think no one's watching? To distant calliope music. They TORMENT her, Titus, it's the CURSE of the CLOWNS. Oom pah pah Oom pah pah!

SIG. *(An outburst.)* Stop! Stop it!

TITUS. Wow. This is so GOOD — where's my pen. Where's my pad.

SIG. Go ask Claude for a pen. GO!!

TITUS. Um. OK. *(He exits. Pause.)*

POLLY. Are you mad?

SIG. You know, Polly, I think I will do another painting of you. While we're all here this weekend.

POLLY. No! No! You won't!

SIG. Yes! Yes, I will! I have everything I need in the TRUNK! Polly — as a little clown schoolgirl. A rusty lunch-bucket beside her and a NOTE in her little white-gloved hand.

POLLY. There is no note in her hand!

SIG. There is so a note in her hand! A note from *Mother!*

POLLY. No!

SIG. A note from Mother saying Good-bye, Polly! I'm leaving

27

because I can't stand living with you all anymore!

POLLY. NO! It's a LIE!

SIG. Yes. She told me! She said Sig, you will always be all right. But Polly is different. Polly is damaged —

POLLY. She never —

SIG. And THAT'S why Mother left! Because of YOU! *(Polly hits Sig with a coffee cup.)* Oh, God!

POLLY. Oh shit. Wow.

SIG and POLLY. Dad! "DAD!" Dad! *(Noah climbs down from the roof.)*

SIG. Daddy! Daddy ! She hit me!   POLLY. I hit her!

NOAH. *(Cornered.)* Baby faces smeared with popsicle. Waiting for Daddy to come through the door. Looking for love, for gum, for candy.

SIG and POLLY. What?

NOAH. I'm just remembering how it was to be always surrounded with the overwhelming presence of children.

SIG. Well, isn't that great. But you know, "DAD" some ACTION is called for. Punish her!

NOAH. I don't think Polly needs punishment. Polly needs — what we all need. Help.

POLLY. That's right. I need help.

SIG. Help. I'm bleeding and SHE needs help. Why do you always side with the criminal?

NOAH. Why did your sister hit you? WHY? *(Distracted.)* I'm sensing something — if I can only listen — Understanding ... the sin of Cain. Not IF your Abel, but when. Wow.

SIG. What's he talking about.

POLLY. He's been selected.

SIG. By —

POLLY. Something.

SIG. I need a band-aid — oh God. Get me some ice for my head.

NOAH. *(Bitten.)* Aauugh!

SIG. What IS that!

NOAH. What WAS that!

POLLY. *(At refrigerator.)* No one refilled the ice trays last night!

SIG. A kind of seizure?

NOAH. — I'm being seized, but I don't know by what!

28

POLLY. There isn't any ice! What should I do? What should I do? What should I do? What —

SIG. Shut UP!! Get a can of soda or something cold. MOVE!! *(Polly does.)*

NOAH. Wow. Those look good. Get me one too, Polly. *(Pause.)* Hello, Sigrid. How vivid to see you.

SIG. *(Pressing soda can to her head.)* I don't know why I should be surprised. It's always the same. The same disorder, the same CLUEless greeting — from "Dad" — the same bullshit philosophy when JUSTICE!! is called for! *(Pause.)* You know, Polly, it would serve you right if I just turned right around and left you here.

POLLY. *(Amazed.)* Why — don't — you?

SIG. Yeah. Right. *(Exits.)*

POLLY. What's wrong with her?

NOAH. *(Uncomfortably.)* She's a funny one, your sister. Well, all of my chickens have come home to roost, this weekend. I've got to go finish planting. Want to give me a hand? Grab the gardening tools. Over the hearth in the handbasket.

POLLY. Sure.

NOAH. We'll finish planting the primroses along the easy, winding path to the Dell. Have you seen what I've done, out there? All of those primroses bordering my wild oats? *(He exits unsteadily with garden tools, Polly following.)*

Scene 5

Claude and Lori and Titus enter, in towels.

CLAUDE. Well. Well, well. How did you like the Steam Room? Hot enough for everyone?

LORI and TITUS. Wow, yes!

LORI. It felt wonderful! Now I don't feel like doing anything!

TITUS. Me neither!

CLAUDE. Well, let's not. Let's not do a THING. Let's all sit and

29

relax and we can talk about what came through in the heat. *(They sit down. Claude smiles at Titus. Titus gets up.)*

TITUS. — what's this?

CLAUDE. It's an antique blanket-warmer. I got it at auction upstate. People used to hang their bedding in front of the fire back in the old days. I use it to dry lingerie.

LORI. Seth and I hang our blankets in front of the fire, too. To help keep us warm in the winter. What a nice cozy treat that is! You'd be surprised! Little things make all the difference when you don't have any heat! *(Lori laughs and then Claude laughs.)* But Seth says that the more we go Off-Mainframe the better.

TITUS. Off-Mainframe?

LORI. I'm sorry. I mean, stop depending on the system.

CLAUDE. And when did you meet Seth, Lori?

LORI. Oh, my. We've been together six months now, but it sure feels like longer! You have to come visit! There's a lot to do, but it's so much fun!

CLAUDE. Way up in the woods?

LORI. Oh, yes! Sometimes it's hard, like this winter I tripped in the dark on my way out to the outhouse and I broke my nose — maybe you noticed that it looks a little crooked? I plan on getting it re-set when we can afford to, but, oh, well, that will be the day. But Seth says that the problem with America today is that the mainframe is ANTI-character. — and of course TV — so no one has any ATTENTION SPAN and —

CLAUDE. *(Dreamily.)* When you're ready, I know someone. He's very good!

LORI. What?

CLAUDE. A good nose-man.

LORI. Oh. Anyway, I was just saying that Seth says the MAINframe is just turning out a bunch of eunuchs that can't function for themselves and are forgetting the wisdom of their forefathers. *(Titus wanders over to a group of yellowing photographs.)*

CLAUDE. You know, *I'm* thinking about having something done. Not a full lift, just here, here and here. And here.

TITUS. Who's in the pictures? Family ancestors?

CLAUDE. *(Joining Titus at D. pictures.)* Noah's family ancestors. Aren't they hideous? I mean look at those old photos. Can you

30

believe those whiskers? Some kind of prohibition against shaving. The men too. I can't remember the sect. Truth-seekers. Religious fanatics. And those women with those terrible BUNS. Or their hair just parted in the center and HANGING DOWN like some bedraggled Commune dweller! *(Pause. Lori thoughtfully scratches her armpit. Claude turns brightly to her.)* You know, Lori, you are one of the FEW people I have EVER seen that can pull OFF that look.

LORI. *(Pleased.)* Oh. Thank you.

CLAUDE. — On you, it's — elegant! I mean look at your BONE structure. I would KILL for that bone structure and how old can you possibly be, twenty-SIX or something?

LORI. Twenty-five —

CLAUDE. Just a BABY. And you, Titus, how old can you possibly be —

TITUS. Um, twenty-seven —

CLAUDE. *(Hungrily.)* Two beautiful young people — with nothing but towels between you and happiness. Now, you see I FEEL twenty five. I FEEL it. That's my TRUTH! And I deserve to look it. Since we CAN. Since science can DO that now.

TITUS. Ah, yes. There's quite a few women in the arts and entertainment world who are ironically manipulating their own self-image. *(Pause.)*

CLAUDE. Exactly.

TITUS. Well, I guess I should be —

CLAUDE. Titus, I sense that you are holding energy. Would you like Lori and me to do a release on you?

TITUS. Oh, no, I'm —

CLAUDE. *(Leading him to the daybed.)* You're saying no but I'm getting yes. You lie down right HERE — *(Quickly releases or produces a concealed apparatus.)* — and put your arms through — HERE! young man. *(Titus finds himself laid out on his belly, head and wrists in the troughs of a wooden restraint.)* Lori, you're going to start on his legs.

LORI. Goody!

TITUS. What IS this?

CLAUDE. Well, it's really part of an old stocks that I bought upstate. But doesn't it make a fabulous massage table. *(Claude and Lori are massaging Titus.)* That's right, Lori. You have good hands.

31

TITUS. Ow!

CLAUDE. How is that, Titus?

TITUS. Oh, very nice, thank you —

CLAUDE. Relax. Drift. Surrender. What ever happens is what is supposed to happen. Tell me more about YOU, Lori. What was your CHILDHOOD like.

LORI. Well, there isn't too much to tell. I spent most of my childhood shut in a closet, actually. I think my mother was kind of overwhelmed. She —

CLAUDE. Titus, what I'm doing now is a deep pressure point breakup on your cystic memory centers.

LORI. Um. And I guess that's about all.

CLAUDE. Sorry, Lori. When I'm doing bio-energetic transfer it sometimes takes me out of linear exchange.

TITUS. Ahh. AHHH!

CLAUDE. What. Yes. What. What is that.

TITUS. It's so ... STRANGE! — I just saw — I'm back —

CLAUDE. Where? Holding on to the bars of your crib? Your mother invading the boundaries of your body-space? A priest — waving his member at you — ?

TITUS. A repressed MEMORY — !

CLAUDE. Pre-school — !

TITUS. GRAD school! In GRAD school — Oh God. It was so HUMILIATING! My roommate — he walked IN on me —

CLAUDE. — masturbating — ?

TITUS. — WORSE! WORSE! I was reading — *The Bridges of Madison County!* Oh God. I LIKED it — I liked IT! It was GOOD! It was GOOD!! AAAUUGH!

LORI. I don't understand.

CLAUDE. Go THROUGH it! Go THROUGH it! Breathe! Breathe!

TITUS. *(Sobbing.)* I'm so ASHAMED!

CLAUDE. Yes! Yes! Lori! Go get the Colonial Flogging Stick! Quick! Quick! *(Sig enters. Pause.)*

SIG. *(To Claude.)* Are you trying to wreck my career? I'm just asking.

TITUS. I was only looking for a pen —

SIG. Titus, I think maybe you should put on your PANTS and go out and interview Noah.

TITUS. OK. *(He leaves.)*
LORI. I'm so glad you came in, Sigrid. I want to get to know all of Seth's family. You know, I never had any brothers and sisters, and when you came in, I said to myself, GOODY, because I never had any —
CLAUDE. Sigrid. I cannot stay in this room with you until we clear what you said to me downstairs.
LORI. 'Scuse me, I thought I heard Seth's truck.
SIG. *(To Claude.)* What planet are you on?
CLAUDE. I'm sorry, Lori. I was so taken out by the unresolved issues between Sigrid and myself that I didn't have the focus to hear you.
LORI. Oh, that's all right. I'm that way myself sometimes. Why, sometimes, Seth will be telling me some problem he's having with some new explosive —
SIG and CLAUDE. What?
LORI. I mean some trouble with the gardens, or the crops or the deer — and I won't hear a word he says. Because I'm off in my own head somewhere. *(Distant thunder.)*
CLAUDE. *(Serene.)* My Goodness. You'd think it was God's judgement against New England or something ...

Scene 6

Noah is on the roof, moodily surveying the sky. Seth is outside.

TITUS. *(Climbing out on roof.)* Mind if I sit down?
NOAH. Why not.
TITUS. I'm a reporter for the *New Arts Journal.*
NOAH. *(Perking up.)* Well, let me tell you. Marijuana ... changed my life. In 1971 a mailroom boy at Aetna Life and Casualty gave me a joint. I looked around me. I saw the sky for the first time. I felt the joy of the grass beneath my feet. I heard the birds singing HOLY HOLY HOLY. The radiant sun appeared to me in its true

33

nature for what it truly *was* — a manifestation of Divine Love. Within five years I was a full-blown drug addict. *(Seth walks through underneath with a fragment of a pipe bomb. He is cursing at something invisible.)*

SETH. SHIT you SHIT you stupid fucking SHIT!! *(Exits.)*

NOAH. *(Waves.)* Hey there, Son! I don't regret the years I spent on drugs. The search for consciousness that became a search for a fix but it lead me into the knowledge of what it was — that needed fixing.

SETH. *(Reenters with larger part of pipe bomb.)* Cock-SUCKER son-of-a-BITCH!!!!! *(Exits.)*

NOAH. I met my second wife while I was practicing in a Monastery near Phuket. She was on vacation at the nearby Club Med. We've been together ever since, not easily, nor always happily, but necessarily, nonetheless.

SETH. *(Reentering, with pipe bomb. Insane with rage.)* Fuck-Sucker Mother-Fucker Ass-Wipe! *(Exits.)*

NOAH. *(Meditative and sonorous.)* Now the vessel that is "Me" reaches the end of its turbulent passage and I can see only — open ocean. But you know, lately, just lately, I've felt a certain sort of, oh, what would you call it — well the Hindus called it … "Neti-neti." A kind of numanistic immanence (in lay terms), and I wonder is it possible that I might simply be — borne up? *(Pause.)* Is there anything else you'd like to know?

TITUS. About what?

NOAH. About me. My career. My years of teaching. For the article you're writing.

TITUS. Actually, it's a cover story about your daughter.

NOAH. Oh. Shit. How embarrassing.

TITUS. Can you tell me anything about her?

NOAH. *(Puzzled.)* Not a damn thing. I never understood her, really. As for her art, she hasn't the soul of a painter. Not as I've ever understood painting. That help?

TITUS. I guess so. *(Polly comes into house below and Sig is calling from offstage.)*

POLLY and SIG. Titus — TITUS! Titus — TITUS!

TITUS. Well, I guess I'd better — *(Titus exits roof. A few moments later, Noah exits.)*

POLLY. TITUS! TITUS!

SIG. *(Offstage.)* — Titus! Titus!

TITUS. *(Enters house below.)* Oh, hello —

POLLY. I was just coming to see —

TITUS. I was just going to find — *(Exits.)*

POLLY. — if you wanted to maybe take a walk? Right. Sure. I'm such a pathetic FOOL!

NOAH. *(Enters house below.)* So am I. I thought he wanted to interview me. I never thought to ask why. I just ASSUMED — and why would I. What have I ever done. Professor at a third-rate college, a novelist not only unpublished, but un-written! I feel like I should surrender, but I don't know what and I don't know to whom. Leaves. We're like leaves in autumn, at my age. People drop. People let go. People can't cope. People —

POLLY. People give up. I know. I know. But it's even harder to give up when you're young. Because then you have nothing to do for such a long time! I don't want to give up, "Dad."

NOAH. Then don't. Intoxicate yourself with the illusion that things matter for a few years more.

POLLY. Thanks. That's really inspirational. *(Sits by hearth.)* I want to ask you something. Why did Mommy leave? Was it because of me?

NOAH. *(Slowly.)* Well, I think she left to find — to fulfill — to attempt to — I don't know. She wanted to ride the rails. She rode freight cars. Non-attachment. She felt — God had told her to let you all go. That that was her special destiny. Just like being without her is yours.

POLLY. It still hurts. I still have a hole in me. Where my mother should have been.

NOAH. Don't I know it. My father was a stone-cold bastard. He only had to look at us and we broke down in tears. Why didn't he LEAVE, the Son of a Bitch?

POLLY. *(Tormented.)* Mommy, come back! We need you!

NOAH. *(Tormented.)* Leave, LEAVE! you hateful Son of a bitch —

POLLY. It all hurts so much.

NOAH. Oh, God it never ends! Fathers and sons ... sons and fathers. Is my father to blame for my lost years? Was his father to blame for his? If I still hold him to account it's me, not him, that stands to lose, for he has taken his crimes with him, and … I — am still alive. *(Seth enters with venison haunches, wrapped and tied in a bloody package. Noah and Polly freeze. His speech is offhandedly punctuated by the actions that illustrate his butchering skills.)*

SETH. These deer come down right into our backyard. I've put in a lot of vegetables and they love to raid the garden. It's become a real problem keeping them out. But we've got meat now. So we freeze it we salt it and we dry it. It's not such a big deal when you remember. Boys Chase Squirrels Climbing High. Bleed Cool Skin Clean Hang. First thing after the kill — *(Swings deer onto table.)* — You have to behead it or cut the jugular vein. Lori puts a bowl underneath, and we like to save the blood for sausage. I had to gut this carcass in a hurry, because I hit her in the liver first, and a ruptured organ can be bad news. *(Slashes at the wrapping and demonstrating matter-of-factly. Noah and Polly are transfixed.)* What I do is, I cut off the feet, and turn her on her back. Slit the skin at the breast-bone. Insert your free hand, like this, and press the inner organs down as you continue to cut, all the way to the asshole. Now, if it had been a buck I would have cut off its dick and balls. The biggest nuisance is they carry so many fleas and ticks. *(Looks up.)* I thought maybe we all could have some for dinner. Freeze the rest.

End of Act One

ACT TWO

Scene 1

Early evening, at the end of dinner. Everyone is sitting at the table, picking at remains of venison. Polly and Lori are up, beginning to clear away.

LORI. *(U. of table.)* We have this vegetable garden, it produces a lot, actually, and we started keeping bees, last year, and the goats — we make our own cheese and yogurt, with just two goats, its really enough milk for us and also our neighbors — Seth hunts and we have a trout stream right near the property. Sometimes we go out at five or six in the morning, and fish before breakfast, fish FOR breakfast, I mean. Even ice fishing — there's always something. You'd be surprised. You have to come up.
POLLY. I'd love to!
LORI. The cabin is small, but we have a guest tent, and its really comfortable — Seth and I sometimes sleep in the tent when the cabin gets too stuffy — or just for a change when the mosquitos aren't too fierce, although with netting —
SETH. Lori, can you pass me a little piece of spleen?
LORI. Here you go.
SIG. Wipe your mouth, please, Seth.
SETH. *(Genial.)* Fuck NO!!
ALL. *(As if Seth has said something particularly witty.)* HAHAHA-HAHA! *(Sig stares him down. He wipes his mouth. More laughter.)*
NOAH. Neat! This was good, Seth. Really good.
CLAUDE. I have dessert for us tonight. I hope everyone likes — Apple Strudel!!
ALL. Yum. Wow. Yum. Fun.
LORI. Now, did you use filo for that, Claude? *(Claude looks*

blank. Sig and Polly laugh rudely.) What?

SETH. Lori wants to know where you bought dessert, Claude.

CLAUDE. Oh! Tarte Tatin at Grand Central.

NOAH. I think its so commendable what you're doing up there, Son. Homesteading — getting OFF the SYSTEM. God. It was my life DREAM … We tried to do it — God knows we tried to do it.

SETH. Of course, our life-style, its not really your kind of thing, Noah, its not exactly like living high on the hog or whatever weird mixed ethnic crap Claude brings back from fucking Dean and Delucca! You know, Titus, when we were here before, she brings home warm sushi and chocolate eclairs.

ALL. HOHOHOHOHO!

TITUS. Well, that sounds all right.

CLAUDE. I brought home enough for everybody! Didn't I!

ALL. HAHAHAHAHA!

SETH. *(Genial.)* I mean sushi and ECLAIRS! For Christ's sake! What kind of fucking clue do you fucking need to do the right fucking thing with fucking food combinations! I mean I'm no Martha Stewart —

POLLY. Oh, please don't sell yourself short — the guest TENT?

NOAH. Who the hell IS Martha Stewart? I've heard that name —

LORI. *(Smiling.)* Seth, Noah, the cursing, please — the baby is listening!

SETH. *(Smiling.)* If I want to say fuck I'll say fuck. Get the fuck off my back about it.

SIG. Speaking of Martha Stewart, Seth, I never heard from you about my Christmas present.

SETH. We didn't open it.

SIG. It's October!

SETH. We don't have space to hang any clowns. I mean, I appreciate the thought and all.

SIG. I hope you all realize, that outside of this room I am respected? As an important American Artist? *(They snigger.)* Why don't you SAY something, Titus!

TITUS. Oh, yes. Sigrid Underfinger is becoming a major name —

NOAH. Of course any real painting has been dead since the 1960's. The fifties, even. God. Maybe even the twenties. Don't you think so, Titus?

SIG. *(A private mantra.)* I make money, they do not. I make money, they do not. I make money ...

TITUS. *(To Noah.)* Well, yes — no — I mean — no real painter today cares about "Painting."

SETH. Hey Noah. I brought you a barrel of homemade Whistel.

NOAH. Neat! What's that!

SETH. Oh, it's a traditional grain-alcohol and herb beverage. We make it in the shed and ferment it. Smoother than moonshine. Gives you a great buzz, though. Gimme a hand we'll get it out of the truck. Maybe we'll have a drink, smoke a cigar out on the porch.

NOAH. Terrific. Good, good. *(Noah and Seth exit. Girls perhaps start to move towards clearing table, make coffee.)*

CLAUDE. Titus, let's talk about *you*. You write for an arts magazine?

TITUS. I'm a senior editor. I write about the changing face of the American Arts Scene — The important and necessary tension between the vertical status quo and the subversive underbelly. History and rebuttal. The artist as re-fashioner of the American identity.

CLAUDE. My! That's so important, that sounds really interesting. Could you do me a favor, Honey, my strap seems to be twisted, if you could just reach under there and —

POLLY. *(Lunging.)* Don't touch her! I'll do that! You know Titus, that's really amazing, what you were talking about — that's kind of my field!

SIG. I didn't know you had a field!

POLLY. Well, of course, I do, if you ever bothered to listen, what do you think I've been writing about for five years? *(Rooting around down the back of Claude's shirt.)* Good God, Claude, what IS this —

CLAUDE. It's a bondage-harness. It's like wearing a hair-shirt. It keeps me constantly in a state of acknowledgement of my dark side. It gets tangled. Thanks, Baby.

POLLY. Well anyway, Titus, that's exactly what I've been exploring in my dissertation —

CLAUDE. *(Feeling Titus' arm.)* You work out, don't you —

TITUS. Oh, not for —

CLAUDE. You're kidding — Play around?

POLLY. Titus, I've heard a lot about your magazine. It's consid-

39

ered really important — Isn't it.

TITUS. Getting to be —

POLLY. I mean your issue on the inspiriting self in contemporary painting —

TITUS. *(Claude is groping him under the table.)* Well, trying to — find — a. Hemm. — FIN!-ger. On the — PULSE! Of — the new aes-THET!-ic.

POLLY. I have this paper I wrote in grad school I'd like to show you. It might be interesting for publication.

TITUS. You'd have to send it to my —

POLLY. *(Attempting a flirtation.)* About the Power of Gynaesthesia? — Towards a Crone Aesthetic? disbanding the myth of Female Enmity? —

CLAUDE. How about more wine —

TITUS. Maybe just a —

CLAUDE. Polly, Polly, Polly, look at us! I need to Clear. I just recognized that I became threatened because you were attempting to impress Titus with your intellectual status, and it was actually directed against me. And for a moment, I hated you. Isn't that so human? And poor Titus — Titus, let's just say what we already know. You can have her, me, or both of us. Our hospitality is — Eskimo. Isn't that from Emily Dickinson, Polly?

POLLY. I don't think so.

CLAUDE. Anyway, "Peace?"

POLLY. Oh my God. I'm so embarrassed.

TITUS. Oh, hey — That's all right.

CLAUDE. Do you know what, everybody — I think maybe I'll sidle on up to the Steam-Room and unwind.

SIG. *(Returning from kitchen.)* From what?

CLAUDE. *(Closing in, quietly.)* Titus, have you ever had love with a woman old enough to be your mother?

TITUS. *(Rigid as a rabbit.)* No.

CLAUDE. *(Gentle.)* It might be profound. What is taboo — but a doorway. Did you love your mother?

LORI. Um, maybe —

SIG. *(Riveted.)* Shhhush!!!

TITUS. I'm — adopted. I never knew — my — birth mother.

CLAUDE. *(Gentle.)* I'm a therapist. I'd be happy to be your guide if you want to open your Damage-Package.

TITUS. My — "Damage-Package?"

CLAUDE. Set it free. Set You free.

TITUS. I don't think —

CLAUDE. Well, come on upstairs, anyway. We could just watch a movie.

TITUS. Um, OK. *(Claude exits. Titus exits. Hypnotized.)*

LORI. What just happened?

POLLY. Damn! Oh, shit! I liked him! I liked him! There was something there! I think he liked ME! Didn't you think so, didn't you feel it?

SIG. Well why didn't you DO anything — you just sit there like a DEAF mute while Bride of Frankenstein wrapped him up in her SPIDER web. It's like watching some thousand-year-old vampire in Daughters of Dracula finally making her move —

POLLY. Oh, that's so hateful and misogynistic. Oh, I'm so glad you brought that up. I immediately reconciled myself to FAILURE. Why Why Why Why Why! *(Enter Noah and Seth. Bringing a Whistel jug and glasses. Noah has Apple Strudel.)*

NOAH. *(Glowing.)* Try this Whistel. This is fantastic stuff, Seth. Just fantastic.

SETH. Well, I just collect the berries. Lori is the one that does the actual stomping. That's the hard work!

LORI. It's so much fun! My feet are green for days! *(All consider this.)*

NOAH. Polly? Sig?

SIG and POLLY. No thanks.

LORI. I guess I will.

NOAH. *(Euphoric.)* It's good to have you children about me. I feel — I feel — that the times are coming when we are about to see the world yield into SPIRIT! PEACE on earth — good WILL! I see men — walking on garden paths — women playing on a great lawn — their clothing is loose and hempen — their teeth are sound and their eyes are bright — they are reading! Illuminated manuscripts. Music fills the air. Their discourse is gentle and their hearts are filled with love! They have turned the world into a garden! Their hands are healing. Recreations are many — they paint, they sew, they dance together in gentle winding folkdances — It's coming! I feel it, I know it! *(The girls beam at Noah. Seth has been*

41

listening with mounting outrage and disbelief.)
SETH. That's no vision of HEAVEN! That's a vision of RETIRE-
MENT! You're RETIRED! Good for you — you can sit there and
spend the last social security check in the universe and buy a fucking
ukelele. What about ME!! What about me, FUCKFACE! *(Pause.)*
NOAH. "Son!"
SETH. "Pop!"
NOAH. "Pop!" that's a good one — "Pop" —
SETH and NOAH. HAHAHAHAH!
POLLY. Stop it! Stop it! I don't understand it!
SIG. *(Studying the men.)* They are having fun. Look at their eyes.
Hey. Seth — its not Noah's fault that you're sick of having one pair
of PANTS! Everyone makes their own way in life.
SETH. Yeah, only if they have something to SELL, like their ASS!
YOU traded on SEX to get your start. POLLY's life may be a total
fucking joke, but at least she didn't rely on RICH BOYFRIENDS
to get her through school.
POLLY. That's right!
SIG. *(To Lori, smoothly.)* — my foul-minded siblings are referring
to the financial and emotional support I received from a DARLING
couple that enabled me to get through ART school, and get the
training I needed to have my CAREER. I ADORED them.
POLLY. She PAID you to get out of town and keep away from
her husband.
SIG. *(Slams down her glass.)* Well. Life is choices, Polly. *(Looks
at Noah.)* Right, "Dad?"
NOAH. Hit me with a little more of that Whistel, Seth.
SETH. *(Reasonably, to all.)* At least Polly never peddled her ASS,
is all I'm saying.
SIG. Maybe that's because *Polly* never came to terms with her
weight problem.
POLLY. *(Earnest.)* Well, maybe Polly didn't spend high school
hanging over a TOILET bowl with her FINGERS down her
throat, either! I'm looking for my OWN terms on which to be a
woman. Not just rolling over to a misogynistic society's gynopho-
bic standards. I'm looking for my OWN terms on which to live.
Right, Seth? That's kind of what you're doing, isn't it, Seth?
Looking for your own terms on which to live? We're kind of alike

in that way, aren't we, Seth?

SETH.   Fuck no. I mean, I'm not hiding out behind all this convoluted academic bullshit.

SETH and NOAH.   HAHAHAHA!

SETH.   *(Wheeling on him.)* — just what the fuck are YOU laughing at, Noah — ? *(A tense moment.)*

SETH and NOAH.   HAHAHAHA!

SETH.   *(Expansive. To all.)* Seriously. If things don't change in this fucking country I'm going to lose my land to fucking TAXES. I bought twelve acres of swamp that nobody wanted seven years ago, I put up a house with my own fucking HANDS — I lived in a tent for three fucking YEARS — and they just fucking reassessed it as a residence, charged me for the fucking upgrade — I got to come up with thousands of fucking dollars I don't have —

SIG.   *(Seething.)* Well, did you apply for a fucking HEARING? Did you fucking THINK about putting on a fucking SUIT, and some fucking SHOES and going to the fucking OFFICE of the fucking TAXBOARD like a fucking GROWNUP and cleaning up your FUCKING LANGUAGE AND APPLYING FOR A FUCKING HEARING? *(Pause. Sig moves away from them.)*

NOAH.   No, he's right. He's absolutely right. There is a group of elitist secret societies. Implementing the World Plan. There's a very interesting book I'm reading — just fascinating. It's called. It's called. Oh, what the hell is it called —

SETH.   What societies, Asshole?

NOAH.   Well, Asshole, put on your thinking cap. If I knew, they wouldn't be secret, would they?

LORI.   The Council on Foreign Relations, the Tri-lateral Commission, and The Federal Reserve. *(Pause. All look at her.)*

NOAH.   Neat!

LORI.   Everyone knows that.

NOAH.   We are moving towards global enslavement, and people sense it, even if they can't articulate it.

POLLY.   World government through electronic domination —

NOAH.   Exactly. Look at the technology. I checked out a book on animal husbandry from the damn library, and within three weeks I was getting catalogues from FEED supply companies! Three weeks! Check out the wrong thing and you've got the Feds up your ass —

43

POLLY. Well, that's why all the card catalogues are going electronic. So the government can locate you. Through your fingerprints on the keys or something. If you check out a subversive book. I'm not saying they can do it yet, but soon. They will soon.

NOAH. — why is nobody identifying it — SPEAKING to the transformation of our lives from individuals to modular slaves!

SETH. *(Mildly, but with an edge.)* You know, Noah, your life might actually be improved if you were a modular slave. You've spent the last forty years trying to fucking find yourself. Maybe you should just admit you're lost, and let the totalitarian state GIVE you a fucking function. *(Pause.)*

ALL. HAHAHAHAH! Whew. Ha. My my.

LORI. Why were you reading about animal husbandry, Noah?

NOAH. Oh, just thinking I might try my hand at farming.

SETH. Well, let me tell you "Dad," you don't just "try your hand" at farming.

NOAH. Well not farming, exactly, just a few goats and chickens. A kind of retirement hobby.

SETH. You don't have the energy to farm. Look Noah, you can't just flake out on a dozen chickens starving to death in a henhouse who are depending on you.

NOAH. I know what you're saying. I was only thinking of one or two —

SETH. Goats need milking! Sheep need shearing!

NOAH. Really a couple of chicken is all I —

SETH. You can't just set up some fantasy and walk away from it!

POLLY. Gee, he just got a book out of the library. Can't a man just get a book out of the library?

SETH. NO! He can't just get a book out of the library! Not any book! Not a book that's going to get him started on abandoning some dumb brute creatures on some ramshackle falling down farm! Start a fucking rock collection if you want a retirement hobby.

NOAH. Seth, I feel like this conversation wants to GO somewhere, and I'm just not sure where that place is.

LORI. It sounds like Noah is looking for a way to honor his inner life. *(Everyone looks at her.)* I feel that was the primary message of Gandalf, the grey Wizard, in the *Lord of the Rings*. That has been such an important book in my life. Gandalf's message was, "Dream." *(Silence.)* Well. It's such a lovely night, out. I think I'll go up to the roof and look at the stars. If no one minds. *(Exits. Pause.)*

POLLY. Why isn't it valid, Seth. To have a couple of chickens AND still shop at Safeway. Things aren't all black or white. And there are so many different shades of GRAY. In the search for MEANING as a person. That's all I want. I just want to find out who POLLY is. And I'm prepared for the fact that the search for POLLY may take a lifetime.

SETH. In other words, POLLY is going to be a bum like —

POLLY. Don't use that word.

SIG. Yeah. I forgot. Mom is the only bum in this family.

NOAH. I prefer to call your mother — a — Ho-Bo.

SIG. A ... "Hobo?"

NOAH. Yes. A — Ho-bo. *(Pause.)* Is something wrong? Besides absolutely everything?

POLLY. Oh. Isn't that interesting. Sig paints Clown Hobos. It's kind of an obsession. Isn't it, Sig.

SIG. *(Startled — to herself.)* It's funny, I never thought — I never saw —

POLLY. Rail-riding Hobos. Over and over. And over and over. Two long parallel empty rails, all the way to the horizon. *(To the tune of a song like "Blues in the Night."*)* "Hear that whistle blowing Whooheee — "

SIG. Shut UP! I don't need to take this. I'll be outside if you need me to pay some bills or buy you SHOES or something. *(Sig exits to porch. An awkward silence.)*

POLLY. It's getting so cold already —

NOAH. Well. Shall we all move over to the fire? Bring the strudel, Polly. *(They drift to the hearth. Seth prowling as Noah pokes at the fire.)*

SETH. Hey, "Dad." Isn't this Great-Grandfather's Underfinger's watchmaker's box?

NOAH. Why, yes. Yes it is. I found it up in the attic the other day. And I've been meaning to give it to you, Seth.

SETH. Oh, Man! I haven't seen this for years! I LOVED this thing when I was kid! This is great! Fantastic — with the old

*See Special Note on Songs and Recordings on copyright page.

spring gears —

NOAH. *(Crossing to him, as they admire the box.)* Pinion-wheels — tight as a drum —

SETH. Hair-trigger hand crafted timing pins —

NOAH. Sold brass kleig-fashioned sprocket wrenches —

SETH. Precision-crafted hand-welded eye-pieces —

NOAH. Workmanship like the devil's business —

SETH. Real thing of beauty —

NOAH. Craftsmanship — real Craftsmanship! *(Seth pops it open. Noah, uneasy, moves away.)*

SETH. Hey. What's this? It used to have a million tiny compartments — it was full of all this stuff. The shelves are all gone — where's the insides?

NOAH. I needed something to hold CD's. God I hate the look of those CD holders. All plastic, cheap-shit looking.

SETH. You gutted the insides!

NOAH. I threw so much AWAY when I came back from Asia. I had no room for clutter — in fact I was working on throwing out all the clutter.

SETH. Clutter? Great-Grandfather's watchmaking tools?

NOAH. Well, I'm not saying I did. They're probably around here somewhere.

SETH. How could you do something so STUPID? What the fuck's WRONG with you?

NOAH. Don't you dare talk to me like that in my house —

SETH. That was mine! My past!

NOAH. It was MINE, and if I wanted to throw the damn thing in the fireplace I would!

SETH. My family, my history, you had no right to gut out this box to store your damn CD's!

NOAH. I don't appreciate your — *(Seth is bent over the box.)*

SETH. It's gutted. GUTTED! To hold CD's. They didn't want to buy something plastic, so they took an eighteenth-century watch box and knocked out the insides. All this bullshit about the ANCESTORS and he destroys the only thing worth having from my HERITAGE —

POLLY. *(Nervous.)* From one of our ancestors? Wow!

NOAH. Heritage. A long line of vicious little men with greasy hair

46

and harsh mouths — a corridor of grief, blame, and stony silence broken only by the desolate weeping of women and children. Give me a break.

SETH. No breaks. You don't deserve any breaks. This is a big part of the picture with you, Noah. You have no awareness or respect for anything that's —

NOAH. Did you even listen to what I said? Great-Granddad was a piece of flinty Shit that broke his wife and seven sons. He made his fortune in the Civil War selling telescopes and distance lenses to both sides. He was hated for miles around. There's your precious heritage.

SETH. I don't CARE. Then it IS. I still WANT it. It's my FAMILY!

NOAH. If you want it, welcome to it. I spent my life trying to leave it behind.

SETH. You don't have any respect for what it means to have a family. We had a family that MEANT something. That STOOD for something.

NOAH. *(Sadistically articulate.)* I can tell you that whether through the mercy of age or an act of will, I can now only barely recall any of our bullshit stories about those ancestral visionaries who came to this country hopping, shaking and quaking with the so-called spirit of God. I think I can safely say that based on the few I did know, the best of them were NUTS, but most were FAKES. Beginning with the root stock himself, Great-Great-Grandfather Incremental!

SETH. Incremental Underfinger was a FAKE? FUCK YOU! The man walked with GOD!! GOD had conversations with him. He spoke in tongues! People wrote down what he said when the spirit of prophecy was upon him!

NOAH. Would you like to see what they wrote down? Would you like to hear what he prophesied?

SETH. No, because you'll just twist everything around!

POLLY. Didn't he predict that General Washington was to be killed by a meteor?

SETH. It doesn't mean he didn't know! That he didn't have the gift!

NOAH. He had no gift! He was bitter at being passed over for church appointment. He was meager and spiteful and wanted to punish the whole race of mankind with lingering death for his disappointments in the New World. Because they were turning out to duplicate his disappointments in the old.

SETH. You got a handle on everything, don't you. You got plenty to say about everything, don't you. Know all the right words, don't you.

NOAH. Seth, this conversation seems to want to go somewhere and I'm just not sure where that place is —

SETH. No, "Dad," this conversation is THERE!

NOAH. All right. I have had just about enough from you. I won't be talked to —

SETH. You don't give a shit about ME or the FUTURE or any-one else — all this crap about how fucking HUMANE and Civilized you are — all this I've-been-around-the-world CRAP all over the walls of the house. How much you pay for that crucifix, Noah? And how much for this? *(He brandishes a figurine.)*

NOAH. Don't — that's the Goddess Ho-Dad — worth — *(Seth smashes it on the floor.)* God DAMN it!

SETH. Ho-Dad?

POLLY. Babylonian Goddess of Inertia and Chaos.

NOAH. Jesus Christ, smashed to smithereens. Why the hell did you do that? *(Sig reenters, frightened.)*

SETH. I just liberated you from idolatry. You're just another fuck-ing acquisitions freak, take take take.

NOAH. *(Gathering pieces of statue.)* I wish I had your years and strength again — I'd take you right now. But never mind. We're learning how to do it in laboratories. There are scientists laboring in the secret places of the earth — Harvard, Duke, MIT — who are learning to wind back the clocks of creation — to command the encoded mortality of the cells themselves! And won't children be unnecessary — then!

POLLY. That's awful. What a thing to say.

NOAH. It'll be sweet. As all the bitterness of being pushed aside becomes a thing of the bitter past. Down with the ignominy of old age! I'll take a little pill — and watch the spots and wrinkles reab-sorb — watch myself reconstitute like a dried mushroom! Hello again! My face looks like my face again! To feel luck and energy gathering in these old tin-woodsman's legs — oh, then watch out, my Son — for when we Fathers really rule the world — you'll be the one who's obsolete!

POLLY. Dad! What about your lifelong quest for wisdom and

transcendence? You'd cast your vote with the Bio-Tech boys and live forever?

NOAH. Who wouldn't! You would TOO! The world to come is this world for keeps! Do you think I like having this shrivelled up old pot of a belly? These sinking ribs? Do you think I look at these freaky patches of white standing out of my ears and say — Yeah! That's me! NO! I see that something is horribly wrong. I see my essence waning. Then I look at him in his terrible vitality — stomping around here like Frankenstein's Monster in the duck-pond — and I know who he is!

SETH. Who's that, Old-Timer?

NOAH. He is my Life. I feel it and say — he's stolen my horse and he's riding it away — I'm left on foot, a fool that no one looks at any more.

SETH. Look "Dad" all I want from you is an accounting —

NOAH. Oh, SHUT UP! Who do you think you're talking to! Your Daddy from a million years ago? I'm not the same person. Soon I'll be picked up by the heels and smeared across the void like some pissed-off firefly. And let me tell you, it don't look any better close up!

SETH. When Obadiah died the whole house shook — he said —

NOAH. Don't you understand? There's a stranger at my inner doors, walking from room to room — rattling at my organs, stealing my breath. Undoing all the tiny hooks that keep me fastened to myself. I look behind me and it's all a disappearing blur — before me, the shameful terrors to come. And that's on my good days!

SETH. What about God?

NOAH. If religion is a struggle to be a good sport, I'm not, I've lost. I'm grasping at straws, now, and if I could put a pipette in your juggler vein and suck out twenty more years, you'd be on the floor bubbling, my boy, and wondering in amazement at how fast an old man could move.

SIG. Stop it! Just STOP IT! That's not funny.

NOAH. Oh, I do know God at last. It's he who's been snapping at my ass. The Hound of Heaven himself, saying strike home and live another day.

POLLY. Her, Dad, you might as well say her. The female aspect of God is more nurturing.

49

SIG. Except for female lions and tigers, of course, they just sort of GO for it, don't they.

NOAH. Oh, sadness. Oh magnificent and stupid life I've had, that's had me. I don't give a fuck about you, Son, about any of you. How can I. I mean, of course I do, but really. A man's alone in the end. And family fails. Always. I was your entrance-chute into the big bull-ring. That's all. And now the game is all yours. Why did you come back here. What do you expect of me? What is it you all want?

SETH. I guess I got what I came for. *(Seth bangs out. Long silence.)*

SIG. Well. Wasn't this fun. *(Pause.)* Not one of you is fit to lick Norman Rockwell's boots. *(She exits. Pause.)*

POLLY. Dad? Don't you want to go upstairs?

NOAH. No. Go along. I want to keep watch. *(Polly exits. Noah sits alone.)*

Scene 2

Three hours later. A moon-rise. Lori is sitting on the roof.

LORI. *(Singing.)* Come white lady, lady of the shadows, smile down on me and throw down your silver hair —

POLLY. *(Crawls out window.)* What are you doing out here?

LORI. Couldn't sleep. What are you doing out here?

POLLY. Oh, you'll see.

LORI. And I shall climb the web of your tresses, Lady o lady, and you shall take me flying in the cold night air — MMMMmmmm, MMMMmmmm yeah oh —

POLLY. — That's pretty. Is that from *The Hobbit*?

LORI. No, it's from this band Grimalkin. Do you know them?

POLLY. No.

LORI. No one does. They're from North Dakota. *(Sig emerges over the ridgepole.)* — Here comes Sig. I guess she was restless too. I guess she came out for a little company, too. *(Sig's eyes are wide*

50

open. She touches her cheek.) Is — what's the matter with her?

POLLY. She's sleepwalking.

LORI. Oh the poor thing. Should we —

POLLY. Careful! You mustn't startle her — *(They move carefully towards her — Sig is balancing like a child on the ridgepole. She turns up towards the night sky.)*

SIG. Mother? Mother? Catch me!!

POLLY. NOW!! *(They grab her arms. Sig shrieks.)*

POLLY and LORI. It's OK. You're OK! *(They steady her, and sit her down.)*

SIG. Where am I? Oh my GOD!

POLLY. You tried to jump off the roof again.

SIG. Bullshit. I did not. Bullshit.

POLLY. Yes, you did, she tried to jump, didn't she?

LORI. You tried to jump. Oh, you poor thing. I know just how you feel. You see, I spent most of my childhood shut in this closet, because my mother was very busy with all of my uncles. Why, sometimes I got so lonely I used to —

SIG. *(Wildly.)* All right Lori! I've had about all I can take from you!

LORI. What?

SIG. How DARE you compare my VICTORIOUS life with these pathetic NOTES from the — MUSHROOM cellar!!

POLLY. Oh, you've done it now, Lori, she's starting to cry.

SIG. I am not! I'm crying from the depths of my FRUSTRATION that that moonstruck hillbilly can SIT there in a FLOURSACK thinking that we have ANYTHING in common. I'm crying in SCORN!

LORI. *(Hurt.)* It's not a floursack. It's HEMP.

SIG. — I would have PAID to spend my life in your closet — Lori, safe and surrounded by COATS!

LORI. Sig, I finally feel like I'm beginning to get to know —

SIG. Idiots! The day I finally learn to paint — people will freeze in their tracks — their hair will rise like snakes — and HEADS will explode from God's on down. *(She goes inside.)*

LORI. Will she be all right now?

POLLY. Yup. She'll be all right now.

LORI. *(Singing.)* Come to me oh lai-ai-dee, White lady of my dreams — *(A distant rumble, vaguely like an explosion.)* Do you

want me to teach you the words, Polly, and so you can sing too?
POLLY. No. That's all right.

Scene 3

Continuous time. Sig approaches Noah who still sits in the same position in his chair by the fireplace.

SIG. Polly says ... I think I made the whole world up inside my head.
NOAH. Oh, God. I'd never even considered that. I thought that maybe I'd made everything up. But if I was a figment of YOUR imagination instead. It would explain things. It would —
SIG. Oh Daddy! Can't you please just stop!
NOAH. Well, it isn't very likely.
SIG. Can't you — can't you just say, Sigrid, you don't have a mental problem, you're fine?
NOAH. *(Uncertain.)* Of course I could. Sigrid, you don't have a mental problem, you're fine.
SIG. Thank you.
NOAH. Of course that's just what you told me to say. If you *had* made me up that's just what I *would* say —
SIG. *(In despair.)* I will go mad. And you'll all be so pleased with yourselves because you've finally brought me down. Let me ask you something, Daddy. If we're all just each other's imaginary friends, can't we just PRETEND that we matter to each other? Since we've gone through all that effort ... of dreaming each other up, I mean?
NOAH. *(Slowly.)* That's an extraordinary thing you've just said. You've no idea. *(Pause.)*
SIG. Are you going to stay here all night?
NOAH. I thought I might.
SIG. Do you think ... would you like me to stay with you?
NOAH. I think that would be all right. *(Pats the seat beside him.)*

Scene 4

Morning. Kitchen. Sig is working on a large canvas. The light pours through from the east. Lori enters.

LORI. Well, hey there! Thought maybe I'd rustle up some griddlecakes. *(Sig shudders and continues to work.)* Seth hasn't been back all night. I couldn't get to sleep. *(Pause.)* Seth was out all night. He probably had some errands. *(Pause.)* It was hard to get to sleep. Especially under that moon. Whatcha doin?
SIG. Oh, Gee, Lori, I don't know. What does it look like I'm doing?
LORI. Picture?
SIG. Mmm Hmmm.
LORI. Can I ask you something? Why do you talk to me like I'm a dunce? *(Polly enters.)*
POLLY. I can't believe there's no coffee.
LORI. Good morning, Polly.
POLLY. Morning. Look at this — Algae — Spirulina — every damn kind of pond scum or dehydrated lichen or fungus. Oh. I get it — IGUANAS do the shopping!
LORI. Sounds like someone got up on the wrong side of the bed this morning. I bet a few flapjacks'll fix that —
SIG. I have coffee in my overnight bag.
POLLY. Do you? Do you really?
SIG. Mmmm hmm. It's over there.
POLLY. I'm feeling just a touch suicidal MYSELF, this morning.
SIG. Whatever is that supposed to mean, I wonder. *(Polly returns with coffee. Titus enters wearing only his underwear, socks, and glasses, very dishevelled and unsteady.)*
POLLY. Good morning, Titus.
SIG. Good morning, Titus.
TITUS. *(Quietly distraught.)* Oh, terrible! Oh, sight of all this life hath crossed, most terrible!
POLLY. Would you care for some coffee?

53

TITUS. *(Uncomprehending.)* Coffee? — NO — coffee!! What madness took me. What live thing of evil from the deep did leap upon me. *(He stumbles past her. Sig stops painting.)*

SIG. Are you all right?

TITUS. *(A horrible dawn breaks.)* We played — GAMES. Terrible Games. I saw myself. The cloud of dark within me. What land is this, what dread place? It were better I had died in the wild mountains than be seen by the sun or to see — I who can see nothing GOOD AGAIN!! *(He tears at his hair.)*

POLLY. O fearful sufferer, and wouldst thou kill thy living orbs? What God made blind thy will?

TITUS. My eyes, my eyes what are mine eyes to me when naught to be seen was good?

SIG. What's the matter with him?

POLLY. Oedipus. He's Oedipus. He thinks he slept with his mother. Titus! Titus! Snap out of it!

SIG. Oh, please. It's too damn early for Charades.

TITUS. She SAID she was my mother. SHE PROVED IT AFTERWARDS!! It could be TRUE! My mother gave me away in 1972. SHE gave her son away in 1972. She kept calling me BABY — SON — And telling me there is no GOD and there was nothing WRONG with it! AHHH! I know why everyone keeps taking BATHS in this house!! I'm filth filth filth filth filth!!

POLLY. Listen to me. She never gave away a baby. She just likes to imagine. It's a game. She's a therapist!

TITUS. Omai talas ikmouton eis apas —

SIG. Let's just —

POLLY. Shut UP! He is channeling — pure Attic Greek! It's flawless — its —

TITUS. *Ec*tor'de *pros*dawmat *al*exan *dro*iobeb *ek'ei* —

POLLY. *ka*lata *rau*tos-eu *teuk*sesoon *an*drasin *oitot* — ?

TITUS. *hey*san en*it*troi eh*y*eri baw*la*ki —

POLLY. Incredible. Incredible!

LORI and SIG. What??

POLLY. I asked him about the daily life of the women in Priam's household —

LORI. Yes?

POLLY. And he says that they had a very important school for science and architecture —

TITUS. e' *poi-ei*san tha*la*mon kai *daw*ma Kai *au*lenn! Andromache!

POLLY. And that Andromache herself built and designed most of the important structures and handled all of the interior design in the ancient world. That the men served as sort of farm workers and security guards.

TITUS. Kai — Illi*ad*dos ah *Home*ri*ois* — Nikta —

POLLY. The songs of *The Iliad* kept the men amused at night in the male quarters. The Women's epics, more sort of High Art, have been hidden. What else? What else?

SIG. Titus!

POLLY. Leave him alone!

SIG. You're encouraging a psychosis!

POLLY. — GO INTO IT TITUS!

TITUS. Oh, God, pluck out these poor eyes!

SIG. Titus, now listen to me and listen carefully! Even if she WAS your mother, who gives a shit? All this primitive delicacy about INCEST is a thing of the past — You're in AMERICA, Buddy!

TITUS. No!

SIG. Who the hell CARES who you sleep with anymore! This is the twentieth century, not eight hundred B.C.! Wake up and smell the chemicals. In two more years your mother will be a petri dish and a father will be a miniature hard-drive or something. A NEW WORLD, as dreamed by THIS MAN is upon us. *(Unveils her picture. All are stunned.)*

TITUS. Who is it.

POLLY. Who IS it?

SIG. Leonides of Stanford. Twenty-first Century Genetic Engineer.

TITUS. *(Horrified — awestruck.)* My God! I've never seen anything LIKE it!

SIG. Thank you, Titus.

POLLY. What is he holding?

SIG. He has grafted the legs of a bunny onto a chicken. The chicken has just broken a record for the standing broad jump and died. A sacrifice to Science. The mob opposes Leonides. They are preparing to burn him at the stake.

POLLY. *(Tentative.)* Where are the clowns? There ought to be —

SIG. *(Scornfully.)* Leonides of Stanford is not a Clown. He is the

55

FUTURE! It is he that will transform the human race while the rest of you are collecting foodstamps and practicing YOGA!! Maybe it's a form of self-portrait. I suspect it is.

LORI. Why, it IS a self-portrait. That poor dead chicken with the wrong legs sewn on. It even has your expression. You are very good. Oh, Sigrid — I feel so badly that I ever didn't like you — I —

SIG. How funny you are, Lori. See how you make me laugh. Hahahaha. Oh God.

POLLY. *(Consoling.)* NO, you look GOOD!! *(Seth enters. He is torn and filthy. They all stare at him. Pause.)* Oh my God.

LORI. Seth?

POLLY. I guess you were working underneath the truck, huh? Wow. You really smell like smoke. I guess you were smoking underneath the truck, Seth.

SETH. Oh, I just wanted to make my opinions felt, like you suggested, Sigrid. I think it's a step in the right direction.

POLLY. What? What? What's he talking about?

LORI. Your brother — is a patriot. And a warrior.

SETH. A man has to get his message out.

POLLY. I don't get it.

LORI. What don't you GET! HE BLEW SOMETHING UP!

POLLY. Oh, no. I don't think so. Seth, you didn't — did you —

LORI. Sulphur. Gasoline. The smell of freedom. That's the smell of Freedom.

POLLY. He DOES smell like sulphur! What have you DONE! Oh my God!

LORI. Shut UP!! *(They do.)* He only done what was right. Somebody in this country got to grow some balls.

SETH. Lori, go upstairs and get our stuff together. *(She exits.)*

SIG. *(Anguished.)* Who'd you kill, Seth? Who'd you murder, Big Man! You Idiot! Bombing an office building — oh my GOD!

SETH. Stop saying that! I didn't kill anyone! I'm no murderer! I wanted to make sure it would be completely EMPTY. So I torched a fucking CHURCH!

POLLY. What?

SETH. That old white meeting house out on Route 48.

SIG. The QUAKER MEETING HOUSE? He fire-bombed a Quaker Meeting House? Oh, I'm so proud. WHY?

SETH. Because I'm sick of all the bullshit and hypocrisy!

SIG. What?

SETH. All this "sit around and listen to your inner voice — listen to the promptings of your heart!" "Jesus loves the little children and all that jazz" — Right, Noah?

NOAH. *(Enters.)* What's happened?

POLLY. Seth just burned down the Quaker Meeting House on Old Route 48.

NOAH. The Quaker MEETING house? Where you used to go as kids?

CLAUDE. *(Entering.)* Has anybody seen my little boy?

TITUS. No — no — *(He exits to yard, Claude in pursuit.)*

SETH. — Yes! where we used to go as kids! Dad! Dad! I burned it DOWN! What about THAT, Noah?

NOAH. What will we do? What will we do? I know. We'll say we ALL did it. That's true in its way — we DID all do it —

SETH. We didn't all do it! You didn't have the guts! I DID IT. I just grew up! I just circumcised *myself!* The Wampanoag Indians used to live up around us. When the boys came of age, the men took them into a clearing. Their own FATHERS cut these GASHES in their chests. I mean Big Fucking Gashes.

SIG. Oh, Seth. Give it a rest.

SETH. Then they took Rawhide ROPES and knotted them through the wounds. Their own FATHERS did. Tied them to poles and they had to pull it through their own FLESH without crying — they were twelve years old!

NOAH. I give up. Just what is it I'm being reproached with?

SETH. Where were your fucking values — where was my training in fucking MANHOOD!

NOAH. — really, to be BLAMED for not cutting gashes into your chest when you turned twelve. For giving you a BIRTHDAY party instead. Well excuse the shit out of me — to be BLAMED for taking you to FREEDOM-land instead —

SETH. *Freedomland!* Freedomland. Dicking around on the Ferriswheel! See the Phony Saloon shoot-out at six P.M. —

POLLY. You LOVED Freedomland! We LOVED Freedomland!

SETH. You didn't teach me what I needed!

NOAH. To pierce your damn NIPPLES? With a TOMAHAWK?

You can figure that out on your own!

SETH. Forget it. "Dad." You just don't get anything.

NOAH. Well I guess maybe I don't.

POLLY. I know what he's talking about. It's knowing what to do! To be brave! To be anointed as a Warrior! I WANT that!! I never even had the guts to slash my wrists! Oh, a hesitation mark here or there — a failed foray with a rusty straight pin or two —

SIG. Oh shut up Polly. No one wants to hear about your boring, timid little attempts at self-mutilation. Just slash or get off the pot.

NOAH. Seth, you've always blamed me somehow for Mommy. I didn't leave your mother, she left us!

SETH. You should have FORCED her to stay — you should have chained her up — she probably left because you didn't let her know she HAD to — she couldn't just drop her children like a some kind of litter on the side of the road — what was the matter with you?

SIG. Well. I didn't want to say anything, Seth, but Mommy left because she couldn't stand you. She said —

NOAH. Oh, my son. My son. My son. God, how I love you.

SETH. What? What?

NOAH. My little son.

SETH. ShitHEAD!

NOAH. I look at you and see you in your —

SETH. You do NOT!

NOAH. — pajamas with the crisscrossed baseball bats. Do you remember — ?

SETH. No, fuck you asshole I do fucking not —

NOAH. I can see you right now in those pajamas which you would not take off for love or money —

SETH. Motherfucking asswipe simple SHIT motherfucker —

NOAH. And how we used to say good night — GOOD NIGHT LITTLE SLUGGER —

SETH. FUCK FUCK FUCK YOU — Big Slugger.

NOAH. See you in the sand-pit —

SETH. *(Mysteriously compelled.)* See you in the bull pen —

NOAH. Who can —

SETH. I can —

NOAH. If any man can — Flip Flop Funny Bunny —

SETH. Not my style crocodile —

NOAH. See you in dream-time —

SETH. Love you in the mean-time —

NOAH. 'Night, Son —

SETH. 'Night Dad — Remember to always leave on the night-light —

NOAH. Righty-right! *(Pause.)*

SETH. AAAAH!!! GAAHHH!!! God!! Don't you EVER do that again! You Fuck-fuck-fuck FUCK face!

NOAH. You poor baby. Your cowboys and INDIANS! who beat their wives — and treated them like beasts. That was the legacy of their muscle ripping — training in manhood. Oh. God. It makes me sad. For you to want me to have roughened you somehow by making you bleed, by punching you around — by TOR TURING you — oh my Son, how you must be hurting — how you must be — *(Tries to embrace him.)*

SETH. Hands OFF!! We're MEN now, Noah, at least I am.

NOAH. Well what am I? You think a man doesn't weep, a man doesn't feel — grief, heartache, loss?

SETH. Mother may have walked out the door herself, but YOU packed her suitcase.

POLLY. *(Miserably.)* Bindle. It's called a ...

NOAH. I wanted to support her. Show her there was no anger. That I felt Love.

SETH. Love IS anger. Love is being willing to go to the WALL — Whether you love you family, your country or the human race. Love takes prisoners. Love means being able to say YOU FUCKING ASSHOLE! *(They are quiet.)*

NOAH. Did anyone see you do it?

SETH. No. I'm pretty sure not.

NOAH. Good. That's good. *(They are quiet.)* God. Freedomland. I haven't thought of Freedomland in years. Where was it? In the Bronx?

SETH. Yes.

POLLY. We went almost every year. The last time was on Seth's birthday. Mommy and you had been fighting all morning. The car trip down —

SIG. — was a nightmare.

SETH. No it wasn't. That was a damn good day. It was my birth-

59

day, goddamit.

POLLY. On the George Washington Bridge, Mother says — I woke up this morning and I have absolutely no idea who any of you are.

NOAH. She was a funny one, your mother.

POLLY. She says we never spoke the same language, and she starts to cry — so miserable — so forlorn —

SIG. She says — it's a punishment. I'm like this because I'm being punished. God doesn't exist for people like me. I'm leaving the church. Those people are so angry and repressive.

NOAH. The Unitarians?

SETH. Mommy, what's wrong?

NOAH. Go to Grad school. Major in psychology. Medicine. Literature. Botany!

POLLY. She says what else is there, oh, God isn't there anything else?

NOAH. Just do something! Anything!

SETH. FREEDOMLAND! I see it! There's the sign!

POLLY. Ride an Indian Pony!

SIG. Pocahontas meets the Queen!

SETH. Legends of the Wild West reenacted before your very eyes!

SIG. Great moments in our history — staged every hour! On the hour!

NOAH. We're here.

POLLY. Mother wants to get a boilermaker at the cocktail pavilion.

SETH. What's a boilermaker?

NOAH. Could you just knock it off for the sake of your son, its his birthday in case you've forgotten.

SIG. Mother sulks.

SETH. It's almost High-Noon, time for the Shoot-out at the Easy Saloon!

POLLY. Oh, no — I want to go to the petting Zoo.

SIG. Rowboat on the lake!

NOAH. IT'S SETH'S GODDAM BIRTHDAY and he gets to choose —

SIG. And we make our way, yapping and snapping.

POLLY. I start to sulk, dragging myself behind my family.

SIG. I didn't like my socks, they keep falling into my shoes —

POLLY. — and I've just started to wear glasses, and already I feel the stirrings of my inner Freak, who will blossom so magnificently

60

by sixth grade.

SIG. Keep up. Or I swear to God we're all going home right now. Says our mother.

POLLY. I weep in self-pity.

NOAH. Here's the goddamn saloon.

SIG. Seth. Rapt. Up against the fence.

NOAH. How you doing little Slugger? Happy?

SETH. I'm happy.

SIG. Little Slug — that's his name. Slug. Little Slug. Because Slime comes out of his NOSE. Slug — Ow Polly stepped on my foot really hard!

NOAH. Good for her. Do it again, Polly.

SETH. I HATED the man in black. I wanted to see him DEAD!

SIG. — Don't you know its just a FAKE! Don't you know that its a FAKE? Huh Stupid! They are just guys the PARK HIRED!!

SETH. Shut up. It's NOT!

POLLY. Then Mother starts. "You know the difference, Honey, don't you, between real life and play-acting? An actor PRETENDS to be a certain kind of person — a sheriff, a bank robber, an Indian chief. Someone's daughter, someone's wife — "

SIG. Mommy? We say? Never mind. She says.

SETH. Stop talking! I want to watch!

POLLY. So did I. I was fixated on the man in White — I felt strange feelings — I didn't know what they were — I wanted him to look at my knee where I had scraped it — that thought turned me pink.

SIG. I wanted the man in Black.

NOAH. It was high NOON!

SETH. The man in black was shoving people, hurting them, pushing them into the sides of buildings — he was awful, no one STOPPED him, he walked around the sides of the crowd and his eyes fell on me! He came closer and closer — and Dad said, hold it right there, Pardner —

NOAH. Hold it right there, Pardner!

SETH. — and the man walked on!

SIG . Mother starts laughing — she can't seem to stop.

SETH. Shhh! He's coming, he's coming!

POLLY. The cowboy in the white jacket with the buckskin fringe —

SIG and POLLY. He calls out —

SETH. I think you and me got a little appointment, Black Burt.

NOAH. *They turn, face each other — they count six to draw —* and BLACK BURT *falls dead on the dust — and the children cheer!*

ALL the KIDS. Yay!

SIG. Then we went on the Ferris wheel, Daddy and Seth in one car all together, me, Mommy and Polly in another — and Laugh in the Dark —

POLLY. That was Mother's favorite —

SIG. Then we went home over the George Washington Bridge, and the sun was going down and we had the top down and it was so much better going home —

SETH. I had cotton candy —

POLLY. — drying in cracks all over his mouth — Daddy was humming a little on the way — I had sunburn —

SIG. So did I —

NOAH. And we all started to sing, do you remember? *(Children hum ... happy birthday.)* Oh, it was a golden trip home. We sang Happy Birthday to Seth —

POLLY. And the next morning, Mother was gone. *(Pause.)*

SETH. They shut Freedomland down. I used to pass it on Gunhill Road — a big moldering ruined fairground, you could see RATS running around the rollercoaster tracks. The Ghost town really falling down now. Full of old rubbers and hypodermic needles stuck in the porch of the Easy Saloon. The alligators from the Indian swamp all got loose and died. You can't even see where the canoes used to go. All those townspeople were so terrified that there would be no one to stand up for them. *(Pause.)* Come on, Lori, we've got a long day's driving to do. Good-bye, Dad. *(Claude reenters, leading Titus.)*

LORI. Bye, everyone. Remember to come visit. We have so much fun!

SIG. I'm leaving. Polly — what are you going to do?

POLLY. I don't know, I don't KNOW! I'm all unstrung — I'm confused — I don't know if that was really Oedipus I was speaking to, or some lesser spirit who was lying to HUMILIATE me —

SIG. Don't you understand? It doesn't MATTER.

TITUS. Yeah. Besides, if you're outrageously wrong, you might have a shot at being famous.

SIG. As long as you stay busy. You must work! You must work! No matter how STUPID that work may be.

POLLY. I'll catch a ride with you, Sigrid, but you can drop me at the Y.

NOAH. *(Sees portrait of Leonides.)* Isn't that extraordinary. *(Crosses to it.)*

SIG. *(Flustered, flattered.)* Oh, it's nothing, it's — *(Noah takes portrait D. to light — leans it somewhere, studies it. Sig watches him.)*

TITUS. Polly? Um, if you wanted? You could stay with me. I have an extra room. It's the kitchen, actually, but since I don't ever cook —

CLAUDE. Polly! What fun! Sharing a lover!

TITUS. "Mom," I'm breaking it off.

CLAUDE. Oh, GOD! Oh, GOD! Oh, how you hurt me. Is it because I'm fifty and you're twenty-seven?

TITUS. Yes.

CLAUDE. Well. I'll just have to accept that. Won't I. *(Claude moves to the table. Sig crosses to the door, joining her brother and Lori. Noah stays engrossed in painting. Everyone hovers for a moment, uncertainly.)*

POLLY. Dad? Everyone's leaving … *(He looks up.)*

NOAH. *(Mild, odd.)* Can you imagine being the — last — person to die? Just before the secrets of Eternal Life are discovered in some laboratory at Duke University? Just before we become Gods? Living forever. Just — as we are. Only forever? *(Pause.)* I'm going to think about what — luck — is, now. Good-bye, Children, Good-bye now. *(They begin to exit, as Noah turns back to image of Leonides and the future.)*

ALL. Good-bye —

NOAH. Good-bye —

ALL. Good-bye —

NOAH. Good-bye — *(The lights begin to go down. He looks out. Lights fade to black.)*

End of Play

PROPERTY LIST

Pen and notebook (TITUS)
Suitcase (POLLY)
The Pilgrim's Progress (NOAH)
Sunday *Book Review* (NOAH)
Pancake turner (POLLY)
Bag of chocolate chips (CLAUDE)
Coffee cup (POLLY)
Fragments of pipe bomb (SETH)
Venison in bloody packaging (SETH)
Whistel jug and glasses (NOAH, SETH)
Apple strudel (NOAH)
Watchmaker's box (SETH)
Figurine (SETH)
Coffee (POLLY)

SOUND EFFECTS

Thunder
Distant rumble

NEW PLAYS

• **SMASH by Jeffrey Hatcher.** Based on the novel, AN UNSOCIAL SOCIALIST by George Bernard Shaw, the story centers on a millionaire Socialist who leaves his bride on their wedding day because he fears his passion for her will get in the way of his plans to overthrow the British government. *"SMASH is witty, cunning, intelligent, and skillful."* –Seattle Weekly. *"SMASH is a wonderfully high-style British comedy of manners that evokes the world of Shaw's high-minded heroes and heroines, but shaped by a post modern sensibility."* –Seattle Herald. [5M, 5W] ISBN: 0-8222-1553-5

• **PRIVATE EYES by Steven Dietz.** A comedy of suspicion in which nothing is ever quite what it seems. *"Steven Dietz's ... Pirandellian smooch to the mercurial nature of theatrical illusion and romantic truth, Dietz's spiraling structure and breathless pacing provide enough of an oxygen rush to revive any moribund audience member ... Dietz's mastery of playmaking ... is cause for kudos."* –The Village Voice. *"The cleverest and most artful piece presented at the 21st annual [Humana] festival was PRIVATE EYES by writer-director Steven Dietz."* –The Chicago Tribune. [3M, 2W] ISBN: 0-8222-1619-1

• **DIMLY PERCEIVED THREATS TO THE SYSTEM by Jon Klein.** Reality and fantasy overlap with hilarious results as this unforgettable family attempts to survive the nineties. *"Here's a play whose point about fractured families goes to the heart, mind -- and ears."* –The Washington Post. *" ... an end-of-the millennium comedy about a family on the verge of a nervous breakdown ... Trenchant and hilarious ... "* –The Baltimore Sun. [2M, 4W] ISBN: 0-8222-1677-9

• **HONOUR by Joanna Murray-Smith.** In a series of intense confrontations, a wife, husband, lover and daughter negotiate the forces of passion, lust, history, responsibility and honour. *"Tight, crackling dialogue (usually played out in punchy verbal duels) captures characters unable to deal with emotions ... Murray-Smith effectively places her characters in situations that strip away pretense."* –Variety. *"HONOUR might just capture a few honors of its own."* –Time Out Magazine. [1M, 3W] ISBN: 0-8222-1683-3

• **NINE ARMENIANS by Leslie Ayvazian.** A revealing portrait of three generations of an Armenian-American family. *" ... Ayvazian's obvious personal exploration ... is evocative, and her picture of an American Life colored nostalgically by an increasingly alien ethnic tradition, is persuasively embedded into a script of a certain supple grace ... "* –The NY Post. *"... NINE ARMENIANS is a warm, likable work that benefits from ... Ayvazian's clear-headed insight into the dynamics of a close-knit family ... "* –Variety. [5M, 5W] ISBN: 0-8222-1602-7

• **PSYCHOPATHIA SEXUALIS by John Patrick Shanley.** Fetishes and psychiatry abound in this scathing comedy about a man and his father's argyle socks. *"John Patrick Shanley's new play, PSYCHOPATHIA SEXUALIS is ... perfectly poised between daffy comedy and believable human neurosis which Shanley combines so well ... "* –The LA Times. *"John Patrick Shanley's PSYCHOPATHIA SEXUALIS is a salty boulevard comedy with a bittersweet theme ... "* –New York Magazine. *"A tour de force of witty, barbed dialogue."* –Variety. [3M, 2W] ISBN: 0-8222-1615-9

DRAMATISTS PLAY SERVICE, INC.
440 Park Avenue South, New York, NY 10016 212-683-8960 Fax 212-213-1539
postmaster@dramatists.com www.dramatists.com

• **A QUESTION OF MERCY by David Rabe.** The Obie Award-winning playwright probes the sensitive and controversial issue of doctor-assisted suicide in the age of AIDS in this poignant drama. *"There are many devastating ironies in Mr. Rabe's beautifully considered, piercingly clear-eyed work ... " –The NY Times. "With unsettling candor and disturbing insight, the play arouses pity and understanding of a troubling subject ... Rabe's provocative tale is an affirmation of dignity that rings clear and true." –Variety.* [6M, 1W] ISBN: 0-8222-1643-4

• **A DOLL'S HOUSE by Henrik Ibsen, adapted by Frank McGuinness. Winner of the 1997 Tony Award for best revival.** *"New, raw, gut-twisting and gripping. Easily the hottest drama this season." –USA Today. "Bold, brilliant and alive." –The Wall Street Journal. "A thunderclap of an evening that takes your breath away." –Time. "The stuff of Broadway legend." –Associated Press.* [4M, 4W, 2 boys] ISBN: 0-8222-1636-1

• **THE WAITING ROOM by Lisa Loomer.** Three women from different centuries meet in a doctor's waiting room in this dark comedy about the timeless quest for beauty -- and its cost. *" ... THE WAITING ROOM ... is a bold, risky melange of conflicting elements that is ... terrifically moving ... There's no resisting the fierce emotional pull of the play." – The NY Times. " ... one of the high points of this year's Off-Broadway season ... THE WAITING ROOM is well worth a visit." –Back Stage.* [7M, 4W, flexible casting] ISBN: 0-8222-1594-2

• **MR. PETERS' CONNECTIONS by Arthur Miller.** Mr. Miller describes the protagonist as existing in a dream-like state when the mind is "freed to roam from real memories to conjectures, from trivialities to tragic insights, from terror of death to glorying in one's being alive." With this memory play, the Tony Award and Pulitzer Prize-winner reaffirms his stature as the world's foremost dramatist. *" ... a cross between Joycean stream-of-consciousness and Strindberg's dream plays, sweetened with a dose of William Saroyan's philosophical whimsy ... CONNECTIONS is most intriguing ... Miller scholars will surely find many connections of their own to make between this work and the author's earlier plays." –The NY Times.* [5M, 3W] ISBN: 0-8222-1687-6

• **THE STEWARD OF CHRISTENDOM by Sebastian Barry.** A freely imagined portrait of the author's great-grandfather, the last Chief Superintendent of the Dublin Metropolitan Police. *"MAGNIFICENT ... the cool, elegiac eye of James Joyce's THE DEAD; the bleak absurdity of Samuel Beckett's lost, primal characters; the cosmic anger of KING LEAR ..." –The NY Times. "Sebastian Barry's compassionate imaging of an ancestor he never knew is among the most poignant onstage displays of humanity in recent memory." –Variety.* [5M, 4W] ISBN: 0-8222-1609-4

• **SYMPATHETIC MAGIC by Lanford Wilson. Winner of the 1997 Obie for best play.** The mysteries of the universe, and of human and artistic creation, are explored in this award-winning play. *"Lanford Wilson's idiosyncratic SYMPATHETIC MAGIC is his BEST PLAY YET ... the rare play you WANT ... chock-full of ideas, incidents, witty or poetic lines, scientific and philosophical argument ... you'll find your intellectual faculties racing." – New York Magazine. "The script is like a fully notated score, next to which most new plays are cursory lead sheets." –The Village Voice.* [5M, 3W] ISBN: 0-8222-1630-2

DRAMATISTS PLAY SERVICE, INC.
440 Park Avenue South, New York, NY 10016 212-683-8960 Fax 212-213-1539
postmaster@dramatists.com www.dramatists.com